W9-AEZ-496

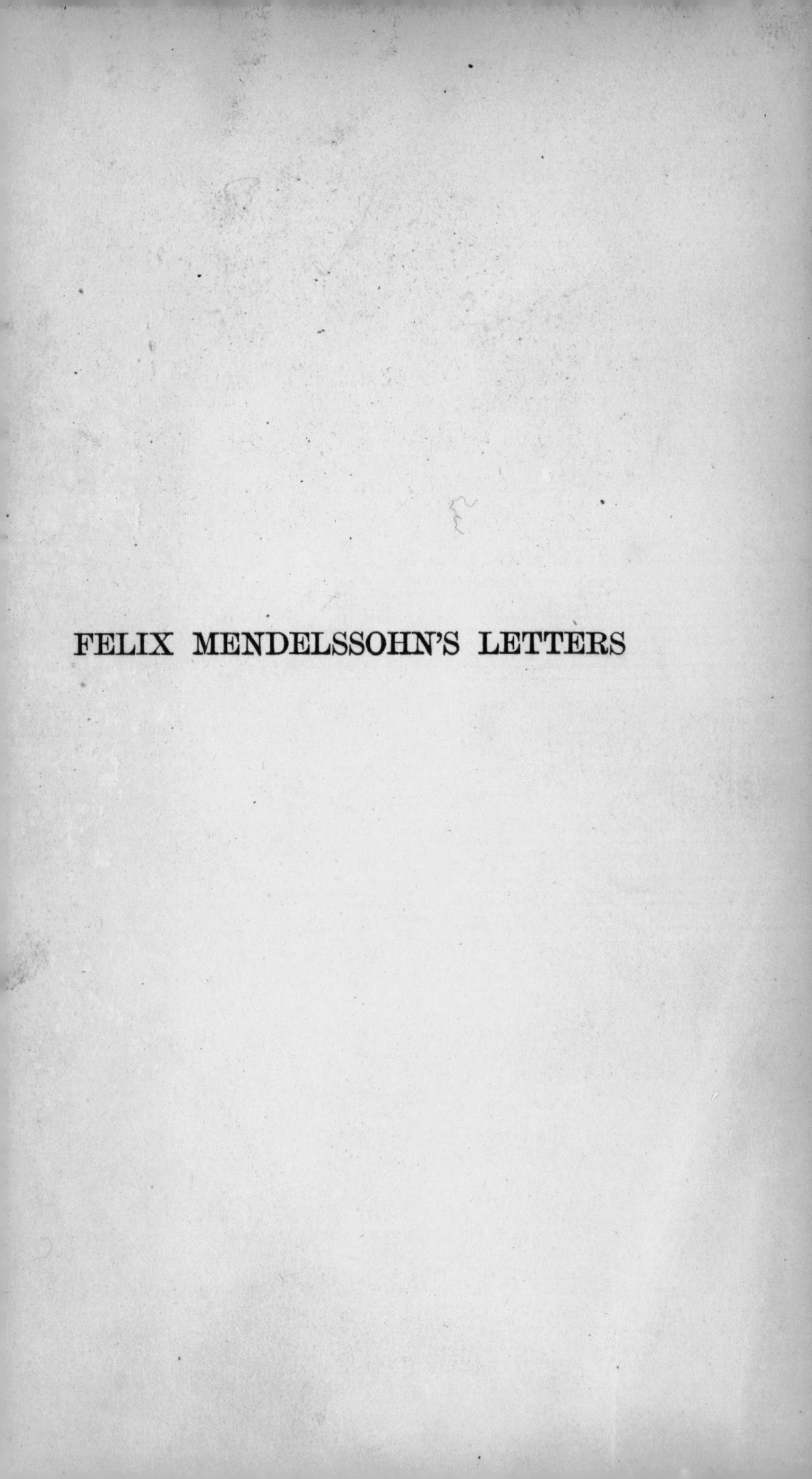

FELIX MENDELSSOHN'S LETTERS

I. Mendelssohn's Study. From a Water-Color made by Felix Moscheles a few days after the composer's death.

LETTERS

OF

FELIX MENDELSSOHN

TO

IGNAZ AND CHARLOTTE MOSCHELES

TRANSLATED FROM THE ORIGINALS IN HIS POSSESSION, AND EDITED

BY FELIX MOSCHELES

ILLUSTRATED

BOSTON
TICKNOR AND COMPANY
211 Tremont Street
1888

University Press:
JOHN WILSON AND SON, CAMBRIDGE, U.S.A.

Dedicated

TO

SIR GEORGE GROVE, D.C.L., LL.D.,

THE TRUEST FRIEND TO MUSIC

AND MUSICIANS.

I AM indebted to Mr. ISAAC HENDERSON, of New York, for his kind assistance in the selections made for publication.

Messrs. LITTLETON, of the firm of Novello, I have to thank for some interesting details in reference to Mendelssohn's business transactions with them.

The letters as published in "Scribner's Magazine," by arrangement, were selections from my manuscript translations. The portraits of Mendelssohn and of the Mendelssohn family were, however, not contributed by me, with the exception of the reproduction of the bust by Rietschel, and of the medallion by Knauer.

FELIX MOSCHELES.

PREFACE.

The letters addressed by Felix Mendelssohn to my father came into my possession in 1870. After Mendelssohn's death, my father had carefully arranged them in a special manuscript book, and had supplemented them with an index of the contents and a table showing the dates of the principal events in the life of his departed friend.

If I have abstained from giving publicity to these letters for so long a time, it is because I thought such delay was in accordance with the wishes of both writers. Many passages occur in which prominent musicians of those days are unreservedly criticised,—passages which I felt as little authorized to suppress as to publish during the lifetime of those alluded to. I trust they will be none the less interesting now that time has judged between the critics and those criticised. Nor did I feel justified in omitting passages that may prove of less interest to the general public than to a smaller circle; for they truly depict the warm friendship which, in the course of years, ripened between Mendelssohn and Moscheles, and they are thoroughly characteristic of the bright and genial way in which Mendelssohn would express his personal feelings.

For a copy of my father's letters to Mendelssohn, I am indebted to Prof. Carl Mendelssohn, of Freiburg, the eldest son of the composer. From these I have made extracts, or embodied their substance in a commentary, where it seemed necessary to explain what Mendelssohn had written. To give them in full I deemed undesirable, so much of similar subject-matter from the pen of my father having already been made public, notably in the "Life of Moscheles," edited by my mother. This biography is chiefly compiled from diaries extending over a period of nearly sixty years, and faithfully reflecting his impressions on the manifold incidents of his artistic career.

The letters addressed by Mendelssohn to my mother could, however, not be omitted, although an English version of most of these appeared in print some years ago. They accompany the letters to my father in chronological order, and bear testimony to the warm regard which Mendelssohn entertained for her, and which she so fully reciprocated. Although only five years his senior, she was well fitted to be his guide and Mentor on his entrance into London society; and he, on his side, was always ready to take advice and friendly hints from his "grandmother," as she would call herself. Since that time half a century has gone by. She has become a grandmother and a great-grandmother, surrounded by a bevy of great-grandchildren; and now, in her eighty-third year, she is still with us, active in mind and body, and, while cherishing the memories of the past, ever ready to share in the joys and to join in the aspirations of the present. And when she looks back on the long list of departed friends, no figure stands out more brightly in her memory than that of Mendelssohn; and we all, young or old, love to listen when she talks of him.

I too have my recollections of him, — juvenile impressions, to be sure, for I was not fifteen when he died; but none the less firmly are they imprinted on my mind. Nor could it be otherwise. From earliest childhood, I looked upon him as my parents' dearest friend and my own specially dear godfather, whose attention I had a right to monopolize, whenever I thought my turn had come. I recollect waiting for that turn more than once, while he was sitting at the piano with my father. When it came, I had every reason to enjoy it. He really was a rare playfellow, a delightful companion, not likely to be forgotten. A certain race across the Regent's Park; the tennis ball thrown into immeasurable space; that pitched battle of snowballs, which appeared to me second to none in the annals of warfare; his improvisation of a funeral march, to which I enacted the part and exemplified the throes of the dying hero, — all seem but things of yesterday. And then the drawing of that troublesome hatchet! — to this day I am grateful to him for helping me with that curve I could not get right. In fact, whether it was play or lessons, my drawing or my Latin, he always took the most lively interest in everything concerning me and my first steps along the path of life, — the thorny path, I might add; for such it was on those occasions when it led me away from the drawing-room in which he was the ever-attractive centre, — when the hour struck which, according to cruel practice, gave the signal for my discreet retirement. It is, however, gratifying to me to remember that I occasionally proved refractory. One evening, in particular, I successfully resisted, when Mendelssohn and my father were just sitting down to the piano to improvise as only they could, playing together or alternately, and pouring forth a never-failing stream of musical ideas. A subject once started, it was caught up as if it were a shuttlecock; now one of the players would seem to toss it up on high, or to keep it balanced in mid-octaves with delicate touch. Then the other would take it in hand, start it on classical lines, and develop it with profound erudition, until, perhaps, the two, joining together in new and brilliant forms, would triumphantly carry it off to other spheres of sound. Four hands there might be, but only one soul, so it seemed, as they would catch with lightning speed at each other's ideas, each trying to introduce subjects from the works of the other. It was exciting to watch how the amicable contest would wax hot, culminating occasionally in an outburst of merriment when some conflicting harmonies met in terrible collision. I see Mendelssohn's sparkling eye, his air of triumph, on that evening when he had succeeded in twisting a subject from a composition of his own into a Moscheles theme, while Moscheles was obliged to second him in the bass. But not for long. "Stop a minute!" said the next few chords that Moscheles struck. "There I have you; this time you have taken the bait." Soon they would seem to be again fraternizing in perfect harmonies, gradually leading up to the brilliant finale, that sounded as if it had been so written, revised, and corrected, and were now being interpreted from the score by two masters.

Bright and enjoyable as were such performances,

they were by no means the only ones that impressed me. In my father's house there used to be a great deal of music-making. "To make music" (*Musikmachen*) is a German expression that covers a vast area of artistic ground. I should say it meant: "To perform music, for the love of music." That is certainly how it was understood by the select little circle of musicians which gathered round the piano in London, and later on in the Leipzig home. Their motto was that which stood inscribed over the orchestra in the Gewandhaus: "Res severa est verum gaudium." High art to them was truly a source of eternal joy. As I write now, I know full well that I was born under a happy constellation; it was a happy name that Mendelssohn had given me, and Berlioz was not wrong when, quoting the line of Horace, he wrote in my album: "Donec eris *Felix*, multos numerabis amicos" (As long as you are *Felix*, you will number many friends). But in those days the fact that I was enjoying special privileges scarcely dawned upon me. It was all a matter of course; to be sure, Mendelssohn or Liszt, the Schumanns or Joachim, would come in and make music, and I would listen devoutly enough many a time; but then, again, I could not always follow my inclinations. There were my Latin and Greek exercises to be done by to-morrow; and when such was the case, I might or might not listen to what was going on in the next room, even if it happened that Mendelssohn was playing and singing some new numbers just composed for the "Elijah."

The mention of my exercises reminds me of an incident truly characteristic of Mendelssohn. It was on the evening of the 8th of October, 1847, memorable to me as being the last I passed in his house. He, Rietz, David, and my father had been playing much classical music. In the course of an animated conversation which followed, some knotty art-question arose and led to a lively discussion. Each of the authorities present was warmly defending his own opinion, and there seemed little prospect of an immediate agreement, when Mendelssohn, suddenly interrupting himself in the middle of a sentence, turned on his heel and startled me with the unexpected question: "What is the *aoristus primus* of τύπτω, Felix?" Quickly recovering from my surprise, I gave the answer. "Good!" said he; and off we went to supper, the knotty point being thereby promptly settled.

But the sounds of mirth, as the chords of harmony, were soon to be silenced. On the following day, the 9th of October, Mendelssohn was struck down by the illness that proved fatal. He died on the 4th of November.

Shortly afterwards I spent many an hour in the house that had been his. Cécile Mendelssohn, his widow, carried her heavy burden with dignity and resignation. The door of his study she kept locked. "Not a pen, not a paper," she says, in a letter to my father, "could I bring myself to move from its place; and daily I admire in him that love of order which, during his lifetime, you have so often noticed. That room must remain, for a short time, my sanctuary,—those things, that music, my secret treasure."

It was with feelings of deep emotion that I entered that sanctuary, when shortly afterwards Cécile Mendelssohn opened its door for me. I possessed already much love for the study of painting; and now I had asked and obtained permission to make a water-color drawing of that room, while all yet stood as the master and friend had left it. There, on the right, was the little old-fashioned piano, on which he had composed so many of his great works; near the window was the writing-desk he used to stand at. On the walls hung water-colors by his own hand,— Swiss landscapes and others; to the left, on the bookcases containing his valuable musical library, stood the busts of Goethe and Bach; on the writing-table, the pen which but the other day was wet, along with this or that object which I had so recently seen in his hand. And as I sat working, doubts and misgivings arose in my mind. Was it not profanation, I thought, to intrude with my petty attempt at painting, where all was hushed in the silence of death? But I worked on, and my thoughts were lost in my first great sorrow. Cécile Mendelssohn came and went. Not a sigh, not a murmur, escaped her lips.

But enough. I close this hasty sketch, although yet many a color and form arise in my memory to complete it. Sufficient has been said in these pages, if between the lines there stands to read, that in editing and translating the following correspondence I have been performing a pleasant duty and a labor of love, and that I feel happy to share with a larger circle of Mendelssohn's friends and admirers the possession of those letters which have so long been dear to me.

FELIX MOSCHELES.

LONDON, *May*, 1888.

LIST OF ILLUSTRATIONS.

2. IGNAZ MOSCHELES

FROM A PAINTING BY FELIX MOSCHELES.

LETTERS

OF

FELIX MENDELSSOHN.

In 1824 Moscheles was engaged on a professional tour, giving concerts in the principal cities of Germany. During his short stay in Berlin, and in response to the two following notes from Mendelssohn's mother, he gave some instruction to Felix, then in his fifteenth year. How fully he, even at this early period of their acquaintance, recognized the genius of the young composer, is shown by an entry in his diary. He says: "I am quite aware that I am sitting next to a master, not a pupil."

Berlin, Nov. 18, 1824.

We much regretted not to see you at dinner to-day; pray let us have the pleasure of your company, if not earlier, at least next Sunday. Have you kindly thought over our request concerning lessons? You would sincerely oblige us by consenting, if you could do so without interfering with the arrangements you have made for your stay in this place. Please do not set down these repeated requests to indiscretion, but attribute them solely to the wish that our children should be enabled to profit by the presence of the "prince des pianistes."

With sincere regards, yours,

L. MENDELSSOHN BARTHOLDY.

BERLIN, Nov. 23, 1824.

Being uncertain whether my son will find you at home, I write this line to ask if you feel inclined to visit the Sing-Akademie. Felix will at any rate call for you, as his way lies in that direction. If you are disengaged, will you join our family dinner at three o'clock, or, should that be impossible, will you accompany Felix, after the "Akademie" (it lasts from five to seven o'clock), and be one of our small circle at tea?

If I may be allowed to renew my request that you will give lessons to my two eldest children, be good enough to let me know your terms. I should like them to begin at once, that they may profit as much as possible during the time of your stay here.

With sincere regard and esteem, yours,

L. MENDELSSOHN BARTHOLDY.

The relative positions of teacher and pupil were soon to be exchanged for friendship of a lasting character, — Moscheles, on the one hand, greeting with the most cordial sympathy the great promises of the youthful genius; Mendelssohn, on the other, appreciating with all the warmth of his artistic nature what had been achieved by the maturer artist, his senior by sixteen years.

In the autumn of 1826 Moscheles, then again on a concert tour through Germany, made a short stay in Berlin, and spent many happy hours with his friends the Mendelssohns. Felix had just completed his Overture to "A Midsummer Night's Dream," and played it, arranged for two performers, with his sister Fanny. Amongst other compositions that mark these early days of his musical career, were the Sonata in E major and an Overture in C. Moscheles in his diary expresses his warm appreciation of those works, and comments at the same time on the fact that "this young genius is so far scarcely recognized beyond the small circle of his teachers and personal friends. One more prophet," he adds, "who will have to lay the foundation of fame in another country."

On the eve of Moscheles's departure from Berlin, Mendelssohn sent him his E major Sonata with the following lines: —

BERLIN, Nov. 28, 1826.

You kindly expressed a wish, dear Mr. Moscheles, to have my Sonata, and I therefore take the liberty of presenting it to you. Should you occasionally come across it, let it remind you of one who will always esteem and respect you.

Once more a thousand heartfelt thanks for the happy hours I owe to your "Studies;" they will long find an echo in my mind. I am sure they are the most valuable of your works, — that is, until you write another.

My best wishes accompany you on what I trust will be a happy and pleasant journey.

Please remember me most kindly to Mrs. Moscheles, and believe me

Ever yours,

F. MENDELSSOHN BARTHOLDY.

During the next two years Mendelssohn was cultivating and developing his natural gifts in every direction. He attended the lectures of Hegel, Ritter, and others at the Berlin University, was in frequent contact with some of the most prominent men of the day, and already took the highest position both as a composer and as a pianist. Amongst the friends who formed the select circle at his father's house, and who remained attached to him through life, were Eduard Devrient, the distinguished actor and writer on Dramatic Art, and Carl Klingemann, who lived many years in England as Attaché to the Hanoverian Embassy. The latter was highly gifted as a poet, and many of Mendelssohn's most popular songs were inspired by his verses.

BERLIN, Dec. 12, 1828.

MY DEAR SIR AND ESTEEMED FRIEND, — My son, in whom you take so kind an interest, is about to leave his home in a few months, and to go forth into the world. He is a musician, and a musician he means to remain; and in furtherance of his musical education he proposes to make some stay in Italy, France, England, and Germany, with a view to becoming acquainted with the great works of art, the prominent artists and art institutions of these countries, and of seeing for himself what Music aspires to, and what it has achieved.

What a comfort it is to us to know that in that vast metropolis, so strange and so new to my son, he is to be welcomed by such true and warm friends as yourself and Carl Klingemann!

To him please remember me most kindly when you see him, and do not fail to present my kindest regards to Mrs. Moscheles.

Yours most truly,

A. MENDELSSOHN BARTHOLDY.

BERLIN, Jan. 10, 1829.

DEAR SIR, — Let me begin by apologizing for troubling you with this letter.

The kindness and friendship you have so often shown me will not, I know, fail me on this occasion; more especially as I come to you for advice on a subject of which I know you to be the most competent judge. The matter on which I want your kind opinion is this:—

I intend to start at the beginning of this year, and to devote three years to travelling; my chief object being to make a long stay in Italy and France. As it is desirable, for several reasons, that I should spend a few days in Berlin about the middle of next December, before leaving for Rome, I intend to devote the eight and a half months of the present year, during which I can absent myself, to visiting first those cities of Germany I am not acquainted with, such as Vienna and Munich, and then, if possible, I would extend my journey to London.

The object I have in view is, not to appear in public, but rather to be musically benefited by my tour, to compare the various views and opinions of others, and thus to consolidate my own taste. As I only care to see what is most remarkable in these two cities, and to become acquainted with those eminent in the world of Art,—not, as I said before, to be heard myself or to appear in public,—I trust the time I can devote to my travels will not prove too short. Now, the question which I want you to decide is this: whether it will be better to begin or to end with London. In the one case I should be in Vienna early in April, remaining there till about the middle of July, and go first to Munich *viâ* the Tyrol, and then down the Rhine to London, where I could stay till December, and return by way of Hamburg to Berlin.

In the other case I should take London first in April, remain till July, then go up the Rhine to Munich, and through the Tyrol to Vienna, and thence back to Berlin. Evidently the former of these tours would be the more agreeable, and as such I would willingly select it; but in following the latter, should I not have a better chance of seeing the two capitals to the fullest advantage,—the season in Vienna coming to an end, as I am given to understand, in May, whereas in London it extends all through June and even beyond?

You, who have so long lived in both cities, and are so well acquainted with musical men and matters in both, will best be able to solve my doubts and to answer a question of so much importance to me. You have given me such constant proofs of your kindness and readiness to oblige, that I feel confident you will not discontinue your friendly assistance, but once more give me the benefit of your advice.

I have yet to thank you for the second book of your splendid "Studies." They are the finest pieces of music I have become acquainted with for a long time,—as instructive and useful to the player as they are gratifying to the hearer. Might you not feel disposed to publish a third book? You know what service you would be rendering all lovers of music. With best regards to Mrs. Moscheles, I have the honor to remain,

Yours most respectfully and truly,

F. MENDELSSOHN BARTHOLDY.

In answer to this and the preceding letter from Mendelssohn's father, Moscheles advises Felix to begin his projected tour with a visit to London.

BERLIN, March 26, 1829.

DEAR SIR,—I sincerely thank you for your kind letter of the 23d of last month, which has quite settled my plans. I shall follow your advice and go to London first. Do not take it amiss if I now recall your kind offers and take you at your word. If I am indiscreet, you have but your own kindness and friendliness to blame; and so I trust you will make allowances for my boldness, and will moreover grant my requests. Your description of London is so attractive, and the way you meet my wishes so friendly, that it is no wonder I made up my mind at once.

According to your advice, I have made inquiries about the boats between Hamburg and London. The first sails on the 4th of April, and after that, one every week. It will be impossible for me to leave by the first or second, as I have hitherto not been able to make any preparations.

I have been very busy lately conducting, for the benefit of a charitable institution, two performances of Sebastian Bach's Passion according to Saint Matthew, with the aid of the Sing-Akademie and the Royal Band; and now the public is loud in its demands for a third performance, which, however, is quite out of the question.

The whole thing has so interfered with the completion of some of my own compositions, and with various business, that I shall require at least a fortnight to prepare for my departure; then I want to stay a few days in Hamburg, so I shall leave only by the third steamer, on the 18th of April, due in London on the 20th. If all goes well, I leave Berlin on the 10th of April, arrive in Hamburg on the 12th, and shall call upon you at your house on the 20th. You cannot fancy how delighted I am at the prospect of seeing you in the midst of your own happy surroundings and in the brilliant position you occupy, and how anxious I am too to hear your latest compositions, especially the new symphony you speak of.

Paganini is here; he gives his last concert on Saturday, and then goes direct to London, where I believe he will meet with immense success, for his never-erring execution is beyond conception. You ask too much if you expect me to give a description of his playing. It would take up the whole letter; for he is so original, so unique, that it would require an exhaustive analysis to convey an impression of his style.

Now, to my great requests; I put them, trusting to your kind indulgence. Can you really take rooms for me, as you suggest in your letter? Anything would be welcome, however small, if in your neighborhood. If so, please let Klingemann know; he would have time to send me the address to Berlin. Secondly, I want your advice as to whether

I should really bring the scores of some of my compositions, and if so, which would be the best to select? I was thinking of my Overture to "A Midsummer Night's Dream;" do you think that suitable? And if I pack manuscripts in my portmanteau, shall I be able to pass the custom-house without difficulty? In that case I would bring several of my compositions, and submit them to your judgment previous to making a selection.

I by no means expect you to answer all my questions yourself, for I know how precious every single moment of your time in London is; but if you will give Klingemann the desired information and your decisions on the above, you will again oblige me, and add one more claim to my sincere gratitude.

Please give my best compliments to Mrs. Moscheles, and believe me

Yours most sincerely,

FELIX MENDELSSOHN BARTHOLDY.

Moscheles writes to say that he has secured rooms for Mendelssohn at No. 203 Great Portland Street, Oxford Street. He urges him to bring with him for performance in London some of his compositions, more especially his Overture to "A Midsummer Night's Dream," and his sixteen-part Cantata, "Hora est," and adds that he will encounter no difficulty at the custom-house.

On the 21st of April Mendelssohn arrived in London; on the 23d Moscheles notes in his diary,

"I took him a round of calls to introduce him to Chappell, Cramer, Collard, etc.;" and then follow daily memoranda, recording pleasant hours spent in and out of Moscheles's house. The following note refers to Mendelssohn's offers of assistance in copying out a Fantasia for pianoforte and orchestra, "Strains of the Scottish Bards," which Moscheles had just written and dedicated to Sir Walter Scott (Op. 80), — a composition which had been put on the programme of Moscheles's concert announced for the 7th of May.

London, April 25, 1829.

Might I request you, dear Mr. Moscheles, to send me by bearer the promised part of your Fantasia to copy? I hope to have some time to spare to-day and to-morrow morning, and will endeavor to distinguish myself to the best of my ability by putting large heads to my notes and being generally correct, so that I may frequently be allowed to assist you; and if you are satisfied with my copying, I trust you will prove it by giving me further orders. I only beg you will send me some sheets of music paper, as I do not know your size and have none by me.

I regret that Professor Rosen,[1] who has just

[1] F. Rosen, Professor of Sanscrit at the London University. He, like Klingemann, was attached to the Hanoverian Embassy, and became an intimate friend of Mendelssohn and Moscheles. His brother, Georg Rosen, himself a distinguished Orientalist, and for many years Consul-General for Prussia in Jerusalem, married Serena, the second daughter of Moscheles.

called on me, has reckoned on my coming to dinner to-day, and I must therefore request you to apologize for my absence to Mrs. Moscheles. At any rate, I shall be with you on Saturday at about eight o'clock, as you have allowed me to do so.

Your respectfully devoted

F. MENDELSSOHN BARTHOLDY.

THURSDAY.

DEAR MRS. MOSCHELES, — I regret that I am engaged for dinner and evening, and see no possibility of getting off, however much I should like it. But I trust you will let me call as soon as I have moved into my Portland Street quarters (I am doing so to-day), and ask when I may come instead. I am much obliged to Mr. Moscheles for desiring to see some of my new things; and if he will promise to let me know when he has had enough of them, I will one of these days bring a cab-full of manuscript and play you all to sleep.

Excuse this hasty line of

Your migrating

FELIX MENDELSSOHN BARTHOLDY.

During the following months they spent many pleasant hours together. Mendelssohn brought the "cab-full;" and amongst other compositions it contained his sacred Cantata on a Chorale in A minor, a Chorus in sixteen parts ("Hora est"), and a stringed Quartet in A minor; and Moscheles finds in the works of the young composer "a solid substratum of study, and the rarest and most promising of natural gifts." He soon became a favorite in all circles of London society, always welcome as an artist and as a genial companion. His Overture to "A Midsummer Night's Dream" was performed, and met with an enthusiastic reception.

What he writes of his Double Concerto is so bright that we quote his own words: —

"Yesterday Moscheles and I had a first trial of my Double Concerto in E in Clementi's piano-manufactory. Mrs. Moscheles and Mr. Collard were our audience. It was great fun; no one has an idea how Moscheles and I coquetted together on the piano, — how the one constantly imitated the other, and how sweet we were. Moscheles plays the last movement with wonderful brilliancy; the runs drop from his fingers like magic. When it was over, all said it was a pity that we had made no cadenza; so I at once hit upon a passage in the first part of the last *tutti* where the orchestra has a pause, and Moscheles had *nolens volens* to comply and compose a grand cadenza. We now deliberated, amid a thousand jokes, whether the small last solo should remain in its place, since of course the people would applaud the cadenza. 'We must have a bit of *tutti* between the cadenza and the solo,' said I. 'How long are they to clap their hands?' asked Moscheles. 'Ten minutes, I dare say,' said I. Moscheles beat me down to five. I promised to supply a *tutti;* and so we took the measure, embroidered, turned, and padded, put in sleeves *à la* Mameluke, and at last with our mutual tailoring produced a brilliant concerto. We shall have another rehearsal to-day; it will be quite a picnic, for Moscheles brings the cadenza, and I the *tutti*."[1]

In the summer of this year Moscheles made a concert tour through Denmark, whilst Mendelssohn took a trip to Scotland with Klingemann. There, after the multifarious duties and pleasures of a London season, he sought fresh strength and energy; there, also, he conceived the germs of two great works, subsequently to be matured, the Scotch Symphony and the Overture to "The Isles of Fingal." Towards the end of November he returned to Berlin, in time for the celebration of his parents' silver wedding.

JAN. 6, 1830.

DEAR MADAM, — I hardly know how to ask your pardon for my sins, for I have a load of them on my conscience; yet were I to trouble you with a string of excuses, you might think that a new sin. To be sure, my writing thus late is unpardonable, considering all the kindness and friendliness you showed me in the spring; but it is true also that these last few days have been the only

[1] The Mendelssohn Family, by Hensel, vol. i. p. 190.

quiet ones since we parted. First, there was our Highland tour in anything but favorable weather, with bad roads, worse conveyances, still worse inns and landlords, and the richest and most picturesque scenery, — all of which so entirely engrossed us that we could not collect our thoughts for even a single day. Then I returned to London; and just as I was finishing some work, and getting through all manner of business before starting for the Netherlands to meet my father, I had the misfortune to be thrown out of a gig, and was obliged to be six weeks in bed and two months in my room. At last I was able to travel home; but my injured foot, which was very weak, made the journey both painful and dangerous, and I felt so prostrate when I did reach home, that I was condemned to another imprisonment of several weeks. A few days ago we celebrated the silver wedding of my parents, for which I was obliged to finish some work;[1] so you see I had a most busy and varied time of it, the happiest and the most disagreeable days of my life following each other in rapid succession. Of course I feel rather upset by all this. Witness this careless, confused letter; yet I would not put off writing lest I should add to my sins.

[1] The *work* alluded to was the Operetta, "The Son and Stranger," in which every member of the family wished to take part. The painter Hensel, who had married Mendelssohn's eldest sister, being totally unmusical, had the part of *one and the same note* composed for him, which even then he was not able to catch.

And now I do not know how to thank you and Mr. Moscheles, for words cannot sufficiently express my gratitude. You know what it is to visit a foreign land for the first time, and to be a stranger among strangers. This feeling, perhaps the most terrible of all others, I have been spared through your kindness, and it is you who have lessened the painful weight of my first separation from my family. If England has made a favorable impression upon me, it is to you I chiefly owe it; and now that I have got over the most difficult part of my tour, I augur favorably for the remainder. I am not going to thank you for each individual act of kindness, or for all the trouble you took about me, — if I did, there would be no end of it; but I may say to you and to Mr. Moscheles that I appreciate from my heart your friendly feelings towards me, and the kindness with which you received me, making all things easy that were difficult to a foreigner. As long as I remember my first entrance into the wide world, so long shall I also remember your goodness. I do not know when I may be so fortunate as to say all this to you instead of writing it down in these formal and cold characters, but I do hope for the pleasure of another meeting before long, and for the continuance of those friendly feelings, for which I shall ever remain

Yours gratefully,

FELIX MENDELSSOHN BARTHOLDY.

Three days later he writes : —

BERLIN, Jan. 9, 1830.

DEAR MR. MOSCHELES, — I have written to Mrs. Moscheles and asked forgiveness for my long silence. Allow me to refer to that letter, and to hope that the reasons therein detailed may plead for me with you; at the same time I cannot refrain from assuring you personally how truly I feel myself indebted to you, and how grateful I am for all the kindness you have shown me. You received me in London in a way I could never have expected, and gave me proofs of confidence and friendship which I shall never cease to be proud of. If hitherto I had looked up to you with admiration, how much more so now, when on closer acquaintance I had the happiness to find in you an example fit, in every respect, to be followed by any artist! You know best yourself the value of a kind reception in a strange country, and the immense advantage of an introduction through you, especially in England. If that country made a most favorable and lasting impression on me, since, for the first time far away from home and friends, I could spend such happy hours, it is you I have to thank, to you I shall always be grateful. Might I but have some opportunity of proving how deeply I feel my obligation! I hope I may soon meet you again in some corner of the world, and find such glorious new pieces of music as I have this time. The Symphony is quite present to my mind, and I can play some of it by heart, especially the first and third movements; but that is very insufficient, and I look forward with impatience to the publication of this masterpiece. Will you not soon give it to the public? You must yourself know how surely you can reckon on a brilliant success and on the admiration and warmest sympathy of every musician. For my part, I should be truly happy to see the score published, and I am convinced that in this feeling I should be joined by all who love music. Will you not soon let a second one follow? Maybe you are at work on one already; it would be truly delightful if you gave us more pieces in the same spirit, imbued with such earnestness and depth; all real lovers of music here would hail them with pleasure.

I mean to leave for Italy as soon as my foot will permit me to travel, and request your permission to write to you occasionally on music and musicians; should your time allow of your sending me a few words, you know how much pleasure it would give me.

With best wishes for your welfare and happiness, and trusting you will preserve a kind remembrance of me, I remain

Yours most sincerely,

F. Mendelssohn Bartholdy.

In the spring of 1830 Mendelssohn started on his continental tour. His first station was Weimar, where, at the urgent request of Goethe, he spent a memorable fortnight in the house of that "Pole-star of poets," as Mendelssohn had described him, when, as a boy of thirteen, he first was privileged to be a guest at his house.

Leaving Weimar, he proceeded to Munich and Vienna, and from there to Italy. On his return he visited Switzerland and several of the German musical centres; and after a short stay in Paris, he once more crossed the Channel, arriving in London in April, 1832. His visit was marked by the most kindly intercourse with his old friends. Speaking of these, he says in a letter to his parents:[1]—

"I wish I could describe how happy I am to find myself here again, where everything is so congenial to my taste, and how glad to meet with so much kindness from my old friends. With Klingemann, Rosen, and Moscheles I feel as much at home as if we had never been separated. They are the centre to which I am constantly gravitating. We meet every day, and I feel thoroughly happy to be with such good and earnest people and such true friends, in whose company I can show myself just as I am, without reserve. The kindness of Moscheles and his wife to me is really touching, and I value it in proportion to my warm and ever-growing attachment to them both."

[1] Mendelssohn's Letters (Reisebriefe), vol. i. p. 357.

During this stay in London he played for the first time his G minor Concerto at the Philharmonic. In Moscheles's concert he conducted his Overture to "A Midsummer Night's Dream," which he had carefully revised, and the Overture to "The Isles of Fingal," recently written at Rome.

Moscheles's birthday was on the 30th of May, and Mendelssohn's congratulations on the occasion of his anniversary took the shape of a drawing humorously illustrating some of his friend's works. "The writing," he says, "is in Emily's hand; the poem, by Klingemann; the design invented, and the ink-blots executed, by Felix Mendelssohn Bartholdy." In his design we find "the young Berliner" (meaning himself) practising a piece that Moscheles had dedicated to him. Further on, "Respect" for the drums, that for once in the way are in tune; the "Blue Devils," that stand for melancholy; "The Last Rose of Summer," on which Moscheles had written Variations; the "Demons" refer to one of Moscheles's "Studies." Next, Moscheles is conducting his Symphony. The Scotchman with his bagpipes illustrates the "Anticipations of Scotland," a piece dedicated to Sir Walter Scott. The stirring theme of the "Alexander Variations" is supposed to bring about the Fall of Paris; and finally, the popular song "Au Clair de la Lune" comes in as being the theme of some brilliant Variations. In the centre of the paper we read:—

3. Mendelssohn's Congratulations to Mosc

Die Schrift ist verfertigt von Emily Moscheles, d. 29sten Mai 1832.
Das Gedicht ist von Carl Klingemann 37 Bury Street St. James
abesken sind erfunden und die Klekse ausgeführt von Felix Mendelssohn Bartholdy
dermal in London

BLAVE TEVFEL

MALINCONICO

Zum
Mai

, der nach oben
iter schreitet,
n oder Loben,
chaffen leitet.

ES B CES
REINGESTIMMT

Respect

3 ani

PLVME, LVNE, CHANDELLE

WIE EIN JVNGER
BERLINER SICH VEBT

on the Latter's Birthday. (See page 20.)

"Hail to the man who upward strives
Ever in happy unconcern;
Whom neither blame nor praise contrives
From his own nature's path to turn."[1]

Mendelssohn spent two months in London, during which time many notes passed between him and the Moscheleses relating to their respective plans and engagements. We translate one of these as showing his attachment to his old master, Professor Zelter, and the simple feeling that prompted him to turn to his friends in his bereavement.

MAY 15, 1832.

DEAR MRS. MOSCHELES, — If you are quite alone at dinner and in the evening, I should much like to come to you. I have just heard of the death of my old master. Please send a line in answer to your

F. M. B.

The next letter is written soon after Mendelssohn's return to Berlin.

BERLIN, July 25, 1832.

DEAR MRS. MOSCHELES, — Pity this is not a note, and the servant waiting below to carry it

[1] Accompanying this translation by Robert Browning was the following tribute to the memory of Moscheles: —

Were my version but as true to the original as your father's life was to his noble ideal, it would be good indeed. As it is, accept the best of
Yours truly ever, ROBERT BROWNING.

to you in an instant, instead of a letter travelling by post, steam, and water, in such a matter-of-fact and business-like way, whereas what I have to say is anything but business-like! I merely long for a chat with you, — a little innocent abuse of the world in general, and a special attack upon phrenology; a weak-fingered pupil, down below in Moscheles's study, playing all the while a slow presto, and being suddenly startled by a few brilliant notes from another hand to relieve her dulness; — in short, I want to go to Chester Place;[1] for if I wish to talk to you, it is you I want to hear and not myself. Now, all these wishes are vain; but why have you strictly forbidden me to thank you ever so little? For that is what I really want to do, but dare not, feeling that you would laugh at me; and after all, there is no way of showing gratitude for happy days. When you look back upon them they are already past and gone, and while they last, you think all the pleasure they bring merely natural; for I *did* think it natural that you and Moscheles should show me all the love and kindness I could possibly wish for. I never thought it might be otherwise; whilst now I do sometimes feel that it was a piece of good fortune, and not a matter of course. All this seems stupid; but if you only knew how strange I have felt these last few weeks, and how unsettled is all I say and think! When I left you on Friday

[1] Chester Place, No. 3, in the Regent's Park, was the Moscheleses' residence.

night to go on board the steamer, I pictured to myself how very much changed I should find our house and the whole family, — two years' absence, married sisters, and so on; but I arrive, and after the first two days, there we are as comfortably and cosily settled as though there had been neither journey, absence, nor change of any kind. I cannot conceive having ever been away; and did I not think of the dear friends I have made meanwhile, I might fancy that I had been but listening to a graphic description of the things and events which I have really witnessed. That, however, would not hold good long, for every step brings some fresh recollection of my journey, which I dreamily pursue, while my thoughts are straying far away; then I am suddenly back again amongst parents and sisters, and with every word they say and every step we take in the garden,[1] another recollection from *before* the journey starts up, and stands as vividly before me as though I had never been away, so that events of all shades get hopelessly mixed and entangled till I am quite bewildered. Whether all this will eventually subside or not, I cannot tell; but for the moment I feel as if I were in a maze and did n't know which way to turn. The past and present are so interwoven that I have still to learn that the past is past. Well, never mind: it was more than a dream; and a tangible

1 The Mendelssohns' house and garden, No. 3 Leipzigerstrasse, Berlin, now form part of the building in which the Reichstag is held.

proof is this letter which, poor as it is, I write and forward to you. You have sometimes forgiven me when I was quite unbearable, and excused me on the score of my so-called genius. To be sure, it was nothing of the kind; but what matters, "if only the heart is black," as the beadle says. (Klingemann must tell you that story if you don't know it.[1])

Only fancy, I have not been able to compose a note since my arrival! That is the cause of my troubles, I think; for if I could but settle down again to work, all would be right. Have n't you got some German or English words for a song which I might compose? Of course for a voice down to C and up to F,[2] and I could play the accompaniment in 1833 on the Erard, with the "slow presto" coming up from below. But I think I could not even write a song just now. Who can sing the praises of the spring when shivering with cold in July, — when the green leaves drop, flowers die, and fruit perishes in summer? For such is the case here. We have fires; the rain pours down in torrents; ague, cholera, and the last decision of the German Diet are the topics of the day; and I, who have played my part at the Guildhall,[3] am compelled to be guarded and concil-

[1] A certain beadle in a country church, being reprimanded by the clergyman for appearing at a funeral in a scarlet waistcoat instead of a black one, retorted, "What matters it, your Reverence, provided the heart is black?"

[2] The compass of Mrs. Moscheles's voice.

[3] Mendelssohn used to delight in attending meetings at the Guildhall to hear Liberal speakers.

iatory lest I should be considered too radical. To-day the cholera is announced again, although not by desire. This Russian gift will, I suppose, settle down amongst us, and not leave us again in a hurry. I am glad there are no quarantine laws, as there were, or else the communications between Hamburg and Berlin might be cut off, and that would be inconvenient to me for certain reasons; though when I first mentioned to your sister in Hamburg that you or Moscheles might possibly come here, I suddenly fell into disgrace. She looked at me very angrily, and asked what was to be got in Berlin, and who took any interest in music *there*. I named myself, but found little favor in her eyes: I was detestable, growing more and more so, the very type of a "Berliner," she thought; next I became a stranger, then yet more, a strange musician; and lastly she turned severely polite. But I changed the subject, remembering your good advice to try and win her favor; so I said that, after all, it was not likely you would go to Berlin, and that quite reconciled her. Secretly, however, I say come—do come! We shall do everything to make Berlin as agreeable to you as it *can* be made; and if Moscheles were to tell me that you intended coming on the 1st of October, I should begin this very day to think of that date with joy. The "Schnellpost-coupé" has just room for two, and it is such easy and comfortable travelling. You should really make up your mind to come. I will not tease you any more to-day, but will only beg you will let me know when you go to Hamburg, that I may write you a letter in sixteen parts, with every part singing out, "Come, do come!"

Of course, I know all the attractions Hamburg has for you, and how difficult it will be for you to tear yourself away. Nothing can be more delightful than your father's new house, looking out, as it does, upon the "Alsterbassin," and the city steeples,— all the rooms so bright and cheerful, amply furnished, and yet not crowded, and no comfort wanting that the most fastidious Londoner could want; besides which, the owner, the rooms, the furniture, and, above all, the large music-room, plainly show how anxiously you are expected. No doubt, then, you will find everything charming and comfortable; but although we have no fine view and no comforts to offer, we should one and all rejoice to see you, and that, indeed, is the main point.

By the by, Madame Belleville is here, and has met with but little success. She intended giving a concert, and the bills announced that Mr. Oury, her husband, was going to assist her; but the Berlin people would not be attracted, so she gave it up, and performed at the theatre between two comedies. People said there was no soul in her playing, so I preferred not hearing her; for what a Berliner calls playing without soul must be desperately cold. Take it all in all, I am *blasé* with regard to Hummel's Septet and Herz's Variations, and the public was quite right to be *blasé* too. Then, again, the "Lovely City" (see Moscheles's unpublished correspondence) is plain, into the bargain, and so I prefer Madame Blahetka. Dear me! how badly I've behaved to her, never saying good-by! Do apologize for me; but, above all, take my part if your sister calls me disagreeable and abuses me for what I said about Berlin. Tell her it was from sheer selfishness I spoke, and that I chiefly thought of my own pleasure in wishing to see you both and the children again,—in fact, say that I'm an egotist, for I am, and do want you to come. My love to Emily and Serena, and may you and Moscheles be as well and as happy as I wish you to be!

Yours,

FELIX MENDELSSOHN BARTHOLDY.

At the close of the London season the Moscheleses went to Hamburg on a visit to Mrs. Moscheles's relatives. The following letter was written on Mendelssohn's hearing of their arrival:—

BERLIN, Aug. 10, 1832.

DEAR MOSCHELES,—

1*st Motto:* "Tell it none but the wise."
2*d Motto:* "Worrying pays."

Old Play.

Therefore I write to you now, for if it pays to worry, worry I will till it would move a stone; and you—tell it none, not even your friends, but come to Berlin. Now look here, since I have your letter from Hamburg I am doubly convinced that come you must, were it but to spend a few days with us here; we will make so much of you! Yesterday I made a thorough inspection of my rooms, and I found that they would suit you splendidly; nowhere else shall you be permitted to take up your quarters than in the Green-score Hotel, Leipzigerstrasse, No. 3, — that is to say, in my room. It faces the street, but it is very quiet and pleasant, and as large as your whole house in Norton Street; and the bedroom next to it is of the same size. I should move a story higher, where another room could be also cleared for servants or any one you choose to bring; a piano awaits you; the stove acts well; in short, you see I am cut out for a house-agent. I really do not exaggerate; you should be comfortably quartered, and all would be well, were not the principal point — your coming — still unsettled. So settle that, and when you do come, let it be to our house; we will have a merry time of it. I should like to send you a fugue in fifteen parts, and the subject of each part should be, "Come to Berlin." True, the country about here is not fine, our theatrical cast not good, no singers worth speaking of, of either sex, but still one can have music.

A thousand thanks for your kind assistance in reference to the "Piano-Songs;" [1] I had already heard from Simrock that you had written to him, and I quite reproach myself for having added one more to

[1] "Klavierlieder," meaning the "Songs without Words." On the copy sent to Moscheles he had called them "Melodies."

the innumerable claims upon your time in London. I cannot sufficiently admire your getting through all you do, with such method and precision; but then, that is just what makes you the "lady patroness" of all musicians who come to London, and it must seem quite hackneyed to you when one of them attempts to thank you for your kindness. Nevertheless, I do so, and thank you with all my heart. You would oblige me by sending me a copy of the "Piano-Songs," as you say you could do so. My father has commissioned his correspondent, Mr. Giermann, to pay you without delay the sum you were so kind as to disburse for me; and now once more accept my best thanks for all the trouble you have taken. The work will certainly go through at least twenty editions, and with the proceeds I shall buy the house No. 2 Chester Place [1] and a seat in the House of Commons, and become a Radical by profession. Between this and that, however, I hope we shall meet, for possibly a single edition may prove sufficient. But what is that allusion to the gravel-pits and the beautiful city? Do you take me for a *damoiseau*, a shepherd, or maybe a sheep? Do you think that I would not hear Madame Belleville because she is not a Bellevue, or because of the wide sleeves she wears? I was not influenced by any such reasons, although I must admit that there are certain faces that cannot possibly belong to an artist, and are so icily chilling that the mere sight of them

[1] Moscheles lived at No. 3 Chester Place, Regent's Park.

sends me to freezing-point. But why should I hear those Variations by Herz for the thirtieth time? They give me as little pleasure as rope-dancers or acrobats: for with them at least there is the barbarous attraction that one is in constant dread of seeing them break their necks, though they do not do so, after all; but the piano-tumblers do not as much as risk their lives, only our ears; and that, I for one will not countenance. I only wish it were not my lot to be constantly told that the public demand that kind of thing I, too, am one of the public, and demand the very reverse. And then she played in the interval between two plays; that, again, I cannot stand. First the curtain rises and I see all India and the Pariahs, and palm-trees and cactuses, and villany and bloodshed, and I must cry bitterly. Then the curtain rises and I see Madame Belleville at the pianoforte, playing a concerto in some minor key, and then I have to applaud violently; and finally they give me "An Hour at the Potsdam Gate," and I am expected to laugh. No, it cannot be done, and there are my reasons why I do not deserve your scolding. I stopped at home because I felt happiest in my own room, or with my friends, or in the garden, which, by the way, is beautiful this year. If you do not believe it, come and see for yourself; that is the conclusion I always arrive at.

I am working on the Morning Service for Novello, but it does not flow naturally; so far a lot of counterpoint and canons, and nothing more. It suddenly crosses my mind that one Sunday evening you did not send me away when I awoke you from a nap at eleven o'clock P. M., but assured me you were not thinking of going to bed yet. That was not right of you; but it also recalls to my mind the Bach pieces we played together, and that leads me to tell you that I have come across a whole book of unknown compositions of the same kind, and that Breitkopf and Härtel are going to publish them. There are heavenly things amongst them that I know will delight you.

Here I have found dreadful gaps; some of the best beloved are missing. I cannot describe to you the feeling of sadness that comes over me when I enter the Academy; it is as though something were wanting in the building, as if it had changed its aspect since those who made it so bright and dear to me are no longer there. Thus the remaining friends are doubly dear, and thus I say, "Come," or rather, "Come, all of you!" for if you come, your people cannot remain in Hamburg, but *must* accompany you; it is but a short journey. You can fancy the loads of kind messages I have to give you and your wife from all my friends, and how they rejoice at the prospect of seeing you here. Above all, I beg of you both not to say a word about this letter to your friends of the Jungfernstieg or the Esplanade; the walls have ears, and if it once got known how selfish I am I should never be able to show myself in Hamburg again.

I meant to write you a short letter, but you know, when we began chatting of an evening, I never noticed how much too late it was getting till your faces grew ceremonious; and as unfortunately I cannot see you now, I must be warned by the paper, and conclude. Farewell, and remember kindly yours,

F. MENDELSSOHN BARTHOLDY.

BERLIN, Sept. 3, 1832.

DEAR MOSCHELES, — Excuse my long silence; I was very unwell at the time I received your last letter, suffering acutely from a musician's complaint, the ear-ache. I meant to write every day, and was always prevented, till at last I am reminded, by Mr. Moore's leaving, how heavily I am in your wife's debt, not having even as much as thanked her for her last letter. Now I feel I must not write to her without also answering your question as fully as I can. Excuse me if I do this in a few words; a proper letter shall follow as soon as I have shaken off that dreadful fit of depression which has been weighing on me for the last few weeks; then only shall I be able to think again pleasantly of pleasant things. Just now I am passing through one of those periodical attacks when I see all the world in pale gray tints, and when I despair of all things, especially of myself. So for to-day, nothing but calculations.

Concerning the concert, I have made inquiries of those in a position to know, and, taking the lowest average, it seems to me you can rely on taking at least one hundred Louis d'or, as I am told that even a tolerably well-attended concert produces that amount, and you can reckon on the presence of the Court, which usually sends twenty Louis d'or to artists of high standing. The time when you ought to give your concert coincides with our Art Exhibition, when Berlin is fullest; it would be the first grand concert of the year, and they say that receipts amounting to one hundred Louis d'or may be expected, and even guaranteed. The cost of the large hall of the theatre is forty Louis d'or, all included (bills, porterage, etc.). The room in the Sing-Akademie is little more than half that sum, but it seems that the Court does not care to go there. The concert-room of the theatre ranks highest, and is considered the most aristocratic; so, at any rate, it would be more advisable for you to take that. All agree on that point. If you deduct forty Louis d'or from the total receipts, there remain, say, sixty Louis d'or. There is no doubt that this is amply sufficient to cover the expenses of posting from Hamburg to Berlin and back, and of making a fortnight's stay with your whole family at the hotel here; and I would not enter into so much detail had not Neukomm mentioned yesterday that when he told you he estimated the net receipts at sixty Friedrich d'or, you thought there would be a risk in undertaking the journey. Let me show you, then, that two post-horses, including fee to post-boy, make one thaler per German mile; so the journey there and back, a distance of thirty-nine miles, and a night's quarters, would come to a little more than one hundred thalers. How you could manage to spend the balance, namely, two hundred thalers, in a fortnight, I cannot see, unless you organized a popular *fête* on a small scale; that, however, probably not forming part of your programme, and your hotel expenses certainly not amounting to more than eight to ten thalers per day, your outlay would surely be covered. According to my estimate, you would have a surplus. To be sure, I admit, unforeseen circumstances might interfere with my calculations; but on the other hand the receipts may be far greater than I have assumed, and at any rate I, for one, have no doubt that your travelling and hotel expenses will be amply covered.

I need not tell you that I give the Berliners credit for sufficient musical taste to expect a crowded concert-room, nor need I say what my wishes on the subject are. The time to come would be between the end of this month and the end of October. The Art Exhibition is then open, and that draws many people to Berlin, and altogether it is the height of our season and the pleasantest time coming.

Now, whatever you decide, let me know without delay, so that in case you do not come, I may leave off rejoicing at the prospect, and that if you choose the better course, — better for us, — I may prepare everything for you to the best of my abilities. In that case I should beg of you to let me know the day of your arrival, date of the concert, etc., and I could get through all the preliminaries, the engagements to singers, and so on, before you were here. But all this is quite understood.

Could you not be induced to accept my offer concerning the use of my rooms? They are large and cheerful enough. I wish you would; but I fear, from what Neukomm said, that the whole plan is already abandoned. Well, I cannot press a matter very strongly that concerns me so closely. I must not be selfish, but wish you to do what seems best to you.

Good-by; remember kindly yours,

F. MENDELSSOHN BARTHOLDY.

Under the same date Mendelssohn writes to Mrs. Moscheles:—

BERLIN, Sept. 3, 1832.

DEAR MRS. MOSCHELES,—That I should have not sooner answered all the pleasant and friendly things you wrote, proves me quite a hardened sinner; but I need scarcely say how happy and grateful I am to receive a letter from you. All else concerning myself is as uncongenial as the "gathering mists." There are times when I should prefer being a carpenter or a turner, when all things look at me askance, and gladness and happiness are so far removed as to seem like words of a foreign tongue, that must be translated before I can make them my own. Such times I have experienced in their dullest shape for the last few weeks. I feel unspeakably dull. And why, you will ask, write all this to me? Because Neukomm last night treated me to a most beautiful lecture that did me no good, and proposed all manner of excellent remedies, which I am not inclined to apply; preached to my conscience, which I can do just as well myself; and lastly asked why I had not yet answered your letter. Because I am in a ferocious mood, said I. But he would have it that one should always write according to one's mood, and that, far from taking it amiss, you would think it the proper thing to do. So it is upon his responsibility I write; and should you be angry, I am a better prophet than he, for I wanted to wait for a more favorable opportunity to send you a cheerful letter, whilst he maintained that the tone mattered little to you.

As for your journey to Berlin, I have written Moscheles a thorough business letter, telling him how matters stand, according to *my* notion and that of others. I will not repeat my request and wish on that score; it might appear selfishness and presumption, both of which I am so thoroughly averse to, that I would avoid even the semblance thereof. If you, however, say your sister has half pardoned me because you are not likely to come here, that is but poor comfort, and I would much rather it were the reverse. You could pacify your sister on your return, and I would give you *carte-blanche* to tell her the most awful things about me, to paint me as black as any negro, for then we should have had you here, and what would all else matter after that?

If Klingemann flirts, he is only doing the correct thing, and wisely too; what else are we born for? But if he gets married, I shall laugh myself to death; only fancy Klingemann a married man! But you predict it, and I know you can always tell by people's faces what they are going to say or to do,—if I wanted bread at dinner, you used to say in an undertone, "Some bread for Mr. Mendelssohn;" and perhaps your matrimonial forecast might be equally true. But, on the other hand, I too am a prophet in matrimonial matters, and maintain exactly the reverse. Klingemann is, and will ever be, a Knight of the Order of Bachelors, and so shall I.[1] Who knows but we may both wish to marry thirty years hence? But then no girl will care to have us. Pray cut this prophecy out of the letter before you burn it, and keep it carefully; in thirty years we shall know whether it proves correct or not.

You want to know how the dresses pleased? But don't you remember it was you who chose them? And need I assure you that they play a prominent part on all festive occasions, and are much admired and coveted? Moreover, a professor of chemistry expressed his astonishment at

[1] Mendelssohn became engaged in 1836, and Klingemann in 1845.

the color of my mother's shawl, scarcely crediting that so beautiful a brown could be chemically obtained. Now, whether everything has been cut right, and according to the latest fashion, I cannot tell; and that is one reason why you should come, just to enlighten me. But, oh! how I should like you to lecture me as you used to do! For how to overcome these fits of intense depression, I really do not know.

Excuse this stupid letter — it reflects the state of my mind — and give my love to all around you.

Ever yours,

FELIX MENDELSSOHN BARTHOLDY.

BERLIN, Sept. 17, 1832.

MY DEAR MOSCHELES, — Excuse my not having answered your letter of the 7th before; I was waiting until I should have something definite to communicate in reference to that plan of yours which I have so much at heart. It was only last night I received some information myself.

First, let me remind you that your wife promised me a good scolding in answer to my crotchety letter and my splenetic mood. I have been keeping savage all this while on purpose, and am still waiting in vain for that most radical of cures. At first I thought that sort of condition was best treated homœopathically, but I find that nothing of the kind does me any good. You see you will have to come yourselves, after all. And that leads me to the following historical particulars.

When I got your letter, I went to Count Redern, the present Director and Autocrat of all dramas and operas, to sound him as you desired. I am on a tolerable footing with him, which means that we esteem one another at a distance. But the noble Count was not to be got at; it was just the time of the manœuvres, and our man of business rode off every morning and received nobody; besides, for that day, a grand extra morning performance was announced for two o'clock, to which all the officers from the camp at Templower Berg were bidden. The civilians — that low set — were only admitted to the pit-boxes, all other seats being occupied by the military. The new opera of "Cortez" was performed, and the sons of Mars applauded mightily; the whole staff was on the alert, and there was no chance of talking to anybody until yesterday, when I at last succeeded in catching the Count. I gave him to understand that you were not disinclined to take Berlin on your way, and to arrange a concert with the authorities of the Opera House, but that you could only remain for a few days. He seemed greatly pleased, as well he might be, and no thanks to him. He said that during your former stay you had given a concert with the Directors of the Opera, and requested me to ask in his name whether the same terms as those stipulated on that occasion, namely, one third of the total receipts, would meet your views. He also proposed one half of the net receipts; but as these much depend on the expenses incurred, which can be made to attain a considerable figure, I advised the other arrangement, especially as the Opera House holds nearly two thousand persons. I begged him to ascertain from the books the exact terms of the former arrangement and let me have them in writing. This document was not completed until last night, and I forward it to you now. It is certain that you can expect good receipts, these however depending more or less on the piece to be acted, and on the general support given by the managers of the theatre. The authorities are always ready with the finest promises; but until the day of your concert is actually fixed, you can expect nothing definite from them.

Now, as you intend going to Dresden or Leipzig, you would actually have to go out of your way to avoid Berlin, and you surely would not treat us so unkindly. And if you care in the least for Serena's pleasure, you must bring her here and let her play with my little nephew Sebastian. Don't imagine that I am forming plans for a matrimonial alliance in that direction; but my nephew is certainly an amiable and well-informed young man of two years of age, whom Serena will love in spite of his paleness and delicacy, for looks of that kind are considered interesting. And then, how happy my two married sisters will be to receive your wife in their homes! How much we will do in honor of you, and how much more for love of you, all that I need not tell you. Come and judge for yourself.

I trust you do not object to my having spoken to Redern without your special instructions. I represented the whole affair, not as a proposal coming from you, but as my own idea and private communication. If you would let me know that you are coming, everything could be so settled that you might arrive on the day itself, if you chose, and leave after the concert. At that, however, I should take offence!

My piano has not yet arrived; I think Erard has forwarded it *viâ* the Equator, or has done something or other, Heaven knows what! Milder tells me her concert is to come off towards the end of October with Neukomm's "Septuor," and a Symphony of his, and some songs of his, and a lot more things of his.

Well, Meyerbeer is formally invested with his title. Were there not a distance of several German miles between a Court Kapellmeister and a real Kapellmeister, it might vex me. The addition of the little word "Court," however, indicates that he has nothing to do, and that again proves the extreme modesty of our nobility; for whenever the word "Court" is put in conjunction with a title, it means that the recipient has the distinction only, not the office, and that he is expected henceforth to rest and be thankful. If they were to make a Court composer of me to-morrow, I should be bound not to write another note as long as I live. I am very glad that Lindenau remembers me kindly. How wicked of me not to have written to him! I really mean to do so shortly, but then you know I am a Court correspondent.

There, I have answered your questions, and now I can give full vent to my wrath and ask you whether you think that I belong to the great brotherhood of grumblers and ought to join their order. Do you presume to laugh at me and my troubles? Imaginary or real, they are intensely worrying; and if, on the one hand, I have had two years of pleasure such as is rarely enjoyed, I have had my full share of misery since. You say I ought to put all that into music. Yes, if it were but so kind as to let itself be put; but it whirls and twirls and shuffles about, and is gone before I can catch it. I hope great things from your wife's scolding, but it has not come yet. I am reading Lord Byron, but he does not seem to do me any good. In short, I do not know what to do. But never mind; good-by.

Yours,

F. MENDELSSOHN BARTHOLDY.

BERLIN, Sept. 26, 1832.

DEAR MOSCHELES!

That's a flourish of trumpets joyfully announcing that you have at last consented to come. It is too delightful to think that we are going to see you and have you here; and what spirits the bare thought puts me in, I need not say. A few lines are enough for to-day; all that is good, the very best, is to come in a fortnight. *Tromba da capo.*

In fact, I only write that you may answer and let me know exactly what I am to do for you here. First, have you quite decided to stay in a hotel (my offer does not seem acceptable to you), and should I not rather take rooms for you by the week? To do so, I ought to know the day of your arrival, and what accommodation you require. Secondly, you speak of putting yourself on good terms with the singers. Have you any special wish that I can communicate to Count Redern in reference to performers or programme? What do you say to having your Symphony performed? but then the whole orchestra should be on the stage, and you should conduct. Thirdly, I will see Count Redern to-day and let him know the good news that you have decided on coming. He must have the newspaper advertisements inserted, and I shall recall to his memory the "appropriate and interesting piece" to be performed. Fourthly, you say: "What piano? that is the question!" I answer: "There be none of Beauty's daughters with a magic like Erard's." Now, my instrument left Hamburg a week ago. I expect it every minute; and as you have already played upon it at your concert in London, I should take it as a great kindness and a good omen if you would inaugurate it here in public. That the instrument is good, you know; so pray say, "Yes." But if perchance you would rather not, then there is my youngest sister's new piano that is to arrive to-morrow or the day after, — a "Graf," which they write wonders about from Vienna. She sends you word that it would be conferring the greatest favor on her, on the piano, and on Mr. Graf, if you would be the first to play upon it in public here. In addition to this, I know for a certainty that all the Berlin pianoforte-makers will besiege your door and go down on their knees to you. There are pear-shaped instruments; there are some with three legs; some with a pedal for transposing and with a small writing-desk inside; some with four strings, others with only one; giraffe or pocket size; black, white, and green. You will have the trouble and toil of selection, so you will have full scope for reflection. Where then is the question?

Now I understand what you say about Music and the great brotherhood of grumblers. Much obliged, but I am not composing at all, and am living much as an asparagus does; I am very comfortable doing nothing. When you come I shall feel quite ashamed at not having anything new to show you; upon my word, I shall not know what to say if you ask me what I have been doing ever since I came here. But, hush! I turn over the paper, and there I encounter the threatening figure of Mrs. Moscheles. Scold, but listen! Do you think that mine is a sort of drawing-room melancholy such as grown-up spoilt children indulge in?

Don't you know that I only wrote so stupidly because I was so stupid? But pardon me, I shall come round again, and by the time you arrive all melancholy will have vanished. You will find neither a discontented creature nor a spoilt child in me, and certainly not a genius; nothing but high spirits will greet you; and, to show that you are not angry, you must at once accept an invitation to a *fête* to be held in my rooms in honor of Moscheles. Several ladies have already promised to come; we will have music, and it will be grand.

A happy meeting then, — but you, O Moscheles, let me have one more answer by letter, and soon after a much nicer one by word of mouth.

Yours,

F. MENDELSSOHN BARTHOLDY.

In a later letter dated Oct. 2, 1832, Mendelssohn recommends the Hôtel de Rome in Berlin. The particulars he gives of the route he advises are characteristic of the mode of travelling in those days.

The journey from Hamburg to Berlin, he says, would take about thirty-four hours. The rooms to be engaged at a hotel are discussed with as much careful insight as the road to be traversed; and then Mendelssohn concludes as follows: —

Count Redern is — a Count, and has gone to his estates, whence he does not return till the 23d. I have not yet been able to catch Arnim, who acts for him during his absence and has been conducting affairs all the summer, but hope to do so tomorrow, when I shall urge upon him to fix the concert no later than the 12th, as you desire.

And now enough of letters, and a happy meeting to all. Love to the children. They shall have sweets, although Emily[1] does prefer Moritz Schlesinger to me. Excuse these hurried lines.

Yours,

FELIX M. B.

Moscheles left Hamburg with his family on the 6th of October, at seven A.M., and arrived the next evening in Berlin, making the journey in thirty-five hours. "Mendelssohn soon joined us at the Hôtel St. Petersburg," he writes, "and complains of being frequently subject to fits of depression." No further mention of such moods is, however, made in the diary. On the contrary, the twelve days of the stay in Berlin are marked by the brightest and liveliest incidents, both social and musical. The "Erard" had at last safely reached its destination; and, Pegasus-like, nobly bore the two friends in willing response to their artistic touch. "The *fête* shall be very grand," Mendelssohn had written, "and we will have music." And so it was; only that instead of one *fête* there were several. The "Hymn of Praise" and some

[1] Emily, Moscheles's eldest daughter, then six years old. She married Mr. A. Roche, of London.

selections from the "Son and Stranger" were performed and admirably rendered by some of the principal singers of the day. Improvisations followed; and no programme was complete without the name of the cherished master, Beethoven.

Moscheles's concert was a brilliant success, the house crowded, and the public enthusiastic; the third part of the receipts, Moscheles's share, was three hundred and one thalers. He left Berlin on the 19th of October. "We dined with Felix at Jagor's," he says; "and when we wanted to say good-by — he had disappeared! At half-past two we were wending our way through a somewhat English fog towards Leipzig, where we arrived next day at noon." There, as in Weimar, Frankfurt, and Cologne, Moscheles played in public or at Court.

On the eve of his departure from Berlin, Mendelssohn presented a most interesting and valuable gift to Moscheles, in the shape of one of those musical sketch-books in which Beethoven was in the habit of jotting down his inspirations as they came to him. These pages, eighty-eight in number, contain chiefly the first ideas for his grand Mass; their appearance can only be described as chaotic, and they are a puzzle even to the initiated. Over one of them the inkstand has been upset; and the master's sleeve, or whatever he may have had at hand, has evidently made short work of the offending pigment. Another page — besprinkled with a few bars here, and a word or two of the Latin text there — is headed: "Vivace. Applaudite amici." The illustration on the next page is a fac-simile of the dedication on the fly-leaf.

In a letter dated November, 1832, Mrs. Moscheles mentions to Mendelssohn that she hears the Philharmonic Society intends commissioning him to write three compositions for one hundred guineas; it is to this that his answer in the following letter refers. She gives him full particulars of her husband's artistic activity, and such news about personal friends as would interest him, and winds up by saying: "Moscheles has just waked from his siesta by the comfortable fireside. You must look upon these pages as if they reflected his dream; for his thoughts, awake or asleep, are constantly with you."

BERLIN, Jan. 17, 1833.

DEAR MRS. MOSCHELES, — How good and kind of you to give me such graphic details! I felt quite happy and cheerful as the fireside, Moscheles's siesta, and the whole establishment, snug and cosy as it is, rose before my eyes. I rejoice like a child at the thought of next spring, of my dignity as a godfather, of green England, and of a thousand things besides. My melancholy is beginning to vanish. I have again taken a lively interest in music and musicians, and have composed some trifles here and there; they are bad, it is true, but they give promise of better things,— in fact, the fog seems lifting, and I again see the

Gegenwärtiges Skizzenbuch L. v. Beethovens
wurde aus der Verlassenschaft desselben
im Dezember 1827 in Wien von mir
erstanden, und unterm heutigen Tag
dem Herrn Felix Mendelssohn-Bartholdy
als ein kleines Zeichen meiner dankbaren
Theil für unvergeßliche Augenblicke, welche mir durch
sein ausgezeichnetes Kunsttalent bereitet
wurden, übergeben.

Wien den 16 September 1830.

Aloys Fuchs.

und aus demselben Grunde (und noch aus vielen anderen) wird
es dann von mir dem Herrn Ignaz Moscheles übergeben
Berlin den 19 October 1832

Felix Mendelssohn Bartholdy

4. Fac-simile of Mendelssohn's Dedication to Moscheles upon the Fly-leaf of Beethoven's Musical Sketch-Book. (See page 48.)

light. Whether I shall be able, after all, to bring some creditable work with me to London, Heaven only knows; but I trust I may, for I would like to figure not only as a godfather, but also as a musician. The former, however, comes first and foremost. I will make the most serious face possible, and bring the very best wishes and all the happiness I can gather together to lay down as a gift at the christening.

And so Moscheles is busy again? Klingemann mentioned a Septet,[1] and I hailed it with delight. What instruments is it for? In what key? Is it fair or dark? He must let me know all about it. And will other honest people be able to play it; or will it be again for his own private use, like the last movement of his Concerto in E flat, which all amateurs stumble over and sigh at without ever being able to master it? Do let me hear all about this Septet; for I am longing to know, and almost envy those who can watch its gradual progress.

I am most truly grateful to the Directors of the Philharmonic for setting me to work for them at the very time I felt so low-spirited and cross-grained. Their invitation to write something came most opportunely. But you don't say whether Moscheles, too, is to compose for them. Will he accept, and what will he write? I will bring my Symphony completed, and possibly another piece, but scarcely a third one.

Do not for a moment think that I am put out

[1] The Septet was written for the Philharmonic Society.

about the Cologne affair. I have enjoyed a good many of the same kind in Berlin that were at first rather bitter to swallow. I know what it is to be a great man amongst the Berliners, now that I am on the eve of my third concert. In the case of my first I had the greatest difficulty to make them accept the whole of the receipts. I played my Symphony in D minor, my Concerto, and a Sonata of Beethoven's, and conducted the "Midsummer Night's Dream." It was crowded, and people were enthusiastic; that is, "heavenly" and "divine" were used much like "pretty well" in ordinary language. And now you should have heard how polite the very people became who had been so obstructive before; how "my noble heart," "my philanthropic views," "my only reward,"—really it deserved to be put into the newspapers. If they had met me kindly at the outset, that would have given me pleasure; now their flow of words is simply a nuisance, and so is the whole place with its sham enthusiasm.

At the second concert we had "Meeresstille." I played a Concerto of Sebastian Bach's, a Sonata of Beethoven's, and my Capriccio in B minor. Madame Milder sang some Scenas by Gluck, and the concert began with a Symphony by Berger. This I put into the programme to please him; but he found its success so short of his expectations, and its execution so bad, that it was only by dint of great exertion that I escaped a complete quarrel with him. At the third concert there will be my

Overture to the "Isles of Fingal," the "Walpurgisnacht," a Concerto of Beethoven's, and a Sonata of Weber's for pianoforte and clarinet, with Bärmann of Munich, — and therewith an end to the honor and pleasure. Excuse all these lengthy details, but indeed there is not much else to report in the way of music. Bärmann has lately given a concert, and enchanted us all (I mean all of us who live in the Leipzigerstrasse, and all Berlin besides). Lafont is shortly expected; Meyerbeer, too. Mademoiselle Schneider has appeared, and with moderate success. Her father is a Kapellmeister, her brother a singer, her uncle a government official, her aunt the wife of the father of the waiting-woman of some princess. That kind of thing is necessary in Berlin. Count Redern has lately taken me under his wing, saying that something might be made of me; so he would patronize me and get me a libretto by Scribe. Heaven grant it may be a good one! but I don't believe it. Besides, we are on the road to improvement, — going to have telegraphs like you! By the by, the two Elsslers — whom they call here "the Telegräfinnen" — are going to London. Should they bring letters to you, and should you have to receive them also, it would make me die with laughter; but present I must be. What will your John say, — he who thought Schröder-Devrient not a lady? And how is Mademoiselle Blahetka? and is Madame Belleville again in London? Spontini wants to sell his instrument for no less than sixteen hundred thalers. If you see Erard, and wish to return him *one* compliment for ever so many, do tell him that my piano is excellent, and that I am delighted with it; for that is the truth.

And now, dear Moscheles, I answer your outside postscript in the same way. Write soon again, and let me hear at full length from you. The Sing-Akademie has not yet chosen a director, and there is as much gossip about it as ever. The Valentins are here for the winter; I see but little of them, as I scarcely go out. Thank you for your list of the Philharmonic concerts. I shall be glad if I can come to the last four; quite out of the question to hear them all. But when is the christening to be? When am I to be a witness to the solemn act? That is the question.

And now I send very best love to all Chester Place, wishing everybody joy and happiness and music, and all that's good in this new year in which we mean to meet again. Until then, and ever, your

FELIX MENDELSSOHN BARTHOLDY.

BERLIN, Feb. 27, 1833.

DEAR MOSCHELES, — Here they are, wind instruments and fiddles, for the son and heir must not be kept waiting till I come, — he must have a cradle song with drums and trumpets and janissary music; fiddles alone are not nearly lively enough. May every happiness and joy and

5. Fac-simile of the Drawing in Mendelssohn's Letter of Feb. 27, 1833. (See page 54.)

blessing attend the little stranger; may he be prosperous, may he do well whatever he does, and may it fare well with him in the world!

So he is to be called Felix, is he? How nice and kind of you to make him my godchild *in formâ!* The first present his godfather makes him is the above entire orchestra; it is to accompany him through life, — the trumpets when he wishes to become famous, the flutes when he falls in love, the cymbals[1] when he grows a beard; the pianoforte explains itself; and should people ever play him false, as will happen to the best of us, there stand the kettledrums and the big drum in the background.

Dear me! but I am ever so happy when I think of your happiness, and of the time when I shall have my full share of it. By the end of April, at the latest, I intend to be in London, and then we will duly name the boy, and introduce him to the world at large. It will be grand!

To your Septet I look forward with no small pleasure. Klingemann has written out eleven notes of it for me, and those I like ever so much.

I can quite imagine what a bright, lively finale they would make. He also gave me a good de-

[1] The German word "Becken" has the double meaning of "cymbals" and "basin."

scription and analysis of the Andante in B flat; but, after all, it will be still better to hear it. Do not expect too much from the compositions I shall bring with me. You will be sure to find frequent traces of moodiness, which I can only shake off slowly and by dint of an effort. I often feel as if I had never composed at all, and had to learn everything over again; now, however, I have got into better trim, and my last things will sound better.

Nice it was, too, that your last letter really found me, as you said it should, alone and in the quiet of my room, composing to my heart's content; and now I only wish that my letter may find you at home on a quiet evening, with your dear ones well and happy around you. We will see whether I am as lucky at wishing as you were. I am in a hurry and must end. I had but half an hour for my letter, and that beautiful picture has taken up all my time; besides, I have nothing further to say but this: I wish you joy now and hereafter, and may we soon meet again. My friends here send their kindest remembrances and congratulations. They are all well but my father, who suffers constantly from his eyes, and is in consequence much depressed; this reacts upon us, and we pray that there may soon be a change for the better. My sister and I just now make a great deal of music, every Sunday morning with accompaniment; and I have just received from the bookbinders a big grass-green volume of "Moscheles," and next time we are going to play your Trio. Farewell, farewell, and remain happy.

Yours,

F. MENDELSSOHN BARTHOLDY.

BERLIN, Feb. 27, 1833.

DEAR MRS. MOSCHELES,—Although I can send you but a few lines to-day, I want to offer you my congratulations, and tell you that I enter heart and soul into your joy at the happy event. How pleased I am to think I shall soon see the little stranger, and that he will bear my name! Do wait till I come, that I may accept your first invitation, and be present in person at the christening. I shall certainly hurry as much as I can, and arrive as soon as possible. I am glad, too, that the new arrival is a boy. He must become a musician; and may all such things as we wish to do and cannot attain be reserved for him! Or if not, it matters little, for he will become a good man, and that is the main point. To be sure, I see already how his two grown-up sisters, Misses Emily and Serena, will tyrannize over him when he is about fourteen years old. He will have to put up with a good deal,—his arms will be voted too long, his coat too short, and his voice wretched. But presently he will become a man and patronize them, doing them many a good turn, making himself generally useful, and submitting to the boredom of many an evening party as their chaperon. I dare say you have somewhat (or should I say greatly) resented my epistolary shortcomings; but do pardon me this once, and I promise to improve, particularly in London, where I can be my own postman and improvise my questions and answers; but I will reform, anyhow.

Kindest messages from my sisters and parents. We all rejoice at the birth of the son.

I must now begin the last movement of my Symphony;[1] it gets into my fingers, spoils my letters, and takes up my time. Excuse, therefore, these hasty lines; how they are meant, you know.

Yours,

FELIX MENDELSSOHN BARTHOLDY.

BERLIN, March 17, 1833.

DEAR MRS. MOSCHELES, — I hope you may not be at home when this letter arrives, and that the future Felix is playing with a rattle or screaming lustily in English, which means that I trust you and the new member of the family are as well as I could possibly wish. Klingemann gave an excellent report in his last letter; and so all I can say once more is, I congratulate you with all my heart.

I can't help thinking that such an important event, such a change in the equilibrium of the whole family and surroundings, such an increase of happiness as well as of cares, must work quite a transformation; and I shall soon come and find

[1] The Italian Symphony.

out for myself whether I am right. But if you do not let me hear that I am mistaken (maybe with a scolding for not writing, or rather for my last bad letter, or with a slight satire on my genius, or something of that kind), I shall feel shy in Chester Place on my first London evening, and timid if I am asked to play to you. Do you happen to be engaged on the 21st of April? If not, I should like to come to you with Klingemann, who is going to call for me, as I fully intend being in London on the 20th. A "Schnellpost" is just driving past, and reminds me that I shall soon sit inside one. Strange to say, since I have begun to work hard, and have become convinced that Berlin society is an awful monster, I should like to remain here some time longer. I feel comfortable, and find it rather difficult to set out travelling again. All the morning there is a constant knocking at my door, but I do not open, and am happy to think what bores I may have escaped, unknown to myself. But when the evening comes and I go round to my parents and we all join in the liveliest discussion and the maddest laughter, then indeed we have a splendid time, and one feels quite reluctant to shorten such hours, not knowing when they shall recur again.

But why write any more? We will talk it all over. I shall have an answer quicker; or rather, it is for me to answer, as I own that you have heaped coals of fire upon my head. I am writing to-day to Moscheles to ask him a favor. I want him to send me one of the many testimonials which, all the year round, he is called upon to give. (It might be lithographed *à la* Smart.) The brothers Ganz, violin and violoncello, wish, after being at Paris, to go to London for the season, if there is a certainty, or at least a chance, of their paying their travelling and other expenses; that is what they want to ask you about, dear Moscheles, and I volunteered to write to you, as my father did for me three years ago. But I have clean forgotten the matter for the last few weeks, and entreat you to send me a few lines for them by return of post; but pray let it be by the very next return, as they are dreadfully offended and have left off bowing to me. And they are quite right, after all, as the time is drawing near.

A most gentlemanly Russian called on me some few days ago, and told me a good deal about Madame Belleville. I wish you could have heard him, dear Mrs. Moscheles. The Russians seem to be more thoroughbred than our Hamburgers. She cannot succeed with them, much as she tries; *she* would, but *they* won't, and all my gentleman had to say about her pretensions and affectation seemed incredible. Anybody passing for affected in Moscow or Petersburg must be so indeed; *that* even the Berlin people allow.

The other day I heard a Berlin pianist play the worst variations on the "God save" that I have

Andante con moto
Wiegenlied
C Klingemann.
Cresc.
Cresc
p
f

6. The "Cradle-Song." (See page 69.)

ever listened to, and that is speaking volumes. The man had great technical ability and good fingers; and yet his performance was hollow and lifeless, and his banging about made me feel miserable. Where in all the world has our Berlin good taste hidden itself? Then again, I have lately heard the "Zauberflöte,"—the best performance, I believe, to be met with nowadays. It is evident that each individual is doing his utmost, that they one and all love the music, and that the only thing wanting is an *ensemble*, which I fear will not be met with in Berlin, as long as sand is sand and the Spree a river. That made me rather melancholy last autumn; but now I look upon things more brightly, and think of the coming spring with its return of warmth and verdure,—that is the best opera one can see and hear. *Au revoir*, then, in the spring.

Ever yours,

FELIX MENDELSSOHN BARTHOLDY.

The spring came, and brought Mendelssohn to London, where he arrived on the 25th of April, 1833. He at once set to work to compose, jointly with Moscheles, a grand Fantasia for two pianofortes and orchestra, which they could bring out as a novelty at the concert announced by the latter for the 1st of May. The theme selected was the "Gipsies' March" from Weber's "Preciosa;" each took his share in the composition of the Variations, and both combined to link them together.

The manuscript score in the two handwritings, with its erasures and additions, its stitchings and patchings, seems to evoke the image of the collaborators, as they worked, thoroughly enjoying the incidents in this joint production.

Moscheles has a few words of graphic description in his diary: "I will make a variation in minor, which shall growl below in the bass," exclaimed Felix; "will you do a brilliant one in major in the treble?" And so it was settled that the Introduction as well as the first and second Variations should fall to the lot of Mendelssohn; the third and fourth, with the connecting Tutti, to that of Moscheles. "We wished to share in the Finale; so he began with the Allegro movement, which I broke in upon with a 'piu lento.' On the night of the concert all went well; not a soul observed that the duet had been merely sketched, and that each of us was allowed to improvise in his own solo, until at certain passages agreed on, we met again in due harmony."

In a letter bearing a later date, Moscheles says: "It is quite amusing to see how people want to find out by which of us this or that variation, this passage in the treble or that modulation in the bass, is written. It is just the intimate fusion of two musical minds that I like; and I tell them that an ice *à la tutti frutti* should not be analyzed otherwise than by dissolving it in one's mouth, and that one should be satisfied with the flavor it leaves behind."

7. First Page of the Original Draft of Mend
original in possession of

"Melodies" (Songs without Words). The
scheles. (See page 66.)

The next note is interesting as having reference to the first book of the "Songs without Words:"

LONDON, in my Club, May 16, 1833.

This morning I again forgot to mention, my dear Moscheles, what I have often intended asking and have as often forgotten,—how matters stand in reference to that publication of mine, and whether there has been any practical result. I have an appointment with V. Novello to-morrow morning; and if he has only sixpence to give me as my share, I would rather not broach the subject. So please leave word at my house whether you think I should mention the matter, or whether it had better rest in eternal oblivion. I return home to-morrow at eleven o'clock to know which way you decide. The saying is: "Merit has its crown;" so I scarcely expect I shall get as much as half a crown.

Yours,

F. MENDELSSOHN.

At Mendelssohn's request to find a publisher for the work, then called "Melodies for the Pianoforte," Moscheles had made arrangements with the firm of Novello, according to which the composer was to receive a royalty on each copy sold. From the books of that eminent firm, we gather that the work was published in 1832, and that on the 11th of June, 1833, Mendelssohn received £4 16*s.* 0*d.*, forty-eight copies being sold. In

1836, four years after the publication, only one hundred and fourteen copies had been disposed of. In 1837 Mendelssohn sold the copyright of the first and third books of "Songs without Words," three Preludes and Fugues for the organ, and three Chorales for female voices, for £35, to Messrs. Novello. We are indebted to Messrs. Littleton of that firm for the original Assignment, which we reproduce.[1] The titlepage is a fac-simile of the manuscript in the possession of Felix Moscheles.[2]

During this stay Mendelssohn conducted his Symphony in A major (the Italian) for the first time, at one of the Philharmonic concerts. At No. 3 Chester Place he was a constant visitor, ever bright and welcome in a circle which included Hummel, Malibran, Paganini, Rubini, Schröder-Devrient, Cramer, etc. On the 17th of May he left for Düsseldorf, to conduct the Musical Festival on the 28th. From there he writes: —

DÜSSELDORF, May 31, 1833.

DEAR MRS. MOSCHELES, — *Meâ culpâ*; but I have been more besieged than ever. I have dropped down on my bed at night unable to write or think, and scarcely able to speak. That sounds touching, but is true, nevertheless; so do not be too angry with me.

This is the first day of leisure, and I write to say that, please God, I shall be back in town on

[1] See Illustration, No. 10. [2] See Illustration, No. 9.

LONDON, Sepr 9th 1837

Memorandum.—**Whereas** I have this day sold to Mr. Joseph Alfred Novello, Music Seller and Publisher, No. 69, Dean-street, Soho-square, at the price or sum of

thirty five pounds ——————

all my Copyright and Interest, present and future, vested and contingent or otherwise, of and in *The Original Melodies Bks 1 and 3 for the P. Forte, also three Preludes and Fugues for the Organ, and also three Choral Pieces for female voices* ——————

composed by me *being Op. 19 38. 37 39 of my works F M B*

And whereas the said sum of *thirty five pounds* ——————

—————— hath been this day paid to me by the said Joseph Alfred Novello, and for which I have given a receipt duly stamped.

Now, in consideration of the Premises and such Payment to me, I hereby, for myself, my executors and administrators, promise and engage to and with the said Joseph Alfred Novello, his executors, administrators, and assigns, at his or their request and cost, to execute a proper assignment of my aforesaid Copyright and Interest to the said Joseph Alfred Novello, his executors, administrators, or assigns, or as he or they shall direct.

Witness my hand, this ninth day of September in the year of our Lord, One Thousand Eight Hundred and thirty seven

Felix Mendelssohn Bartholdy
F M B

Witness {

8. Fac-simile of Assignment to Mr. Novello.

Wednesday the 5th, ready to christen, play, conduct, and even to be a "genius."

All else verbally. So farewell till we meet.

FELIX MENDELSSOHN BARTHOLDY.

Mendelssohn came, this time with his father, christened, played, and conducted, and otherwise kept his word. His first present to his godchild was an autograph album, which he inaugurated with the two pencil drawings reproduced here. The first represents the house in which the Moscheleses lived, — No. 3 Chester Place, Regent's Park. Moscheles himself is supposed to be looking out of the window of his dressing-room. The second is a view taken in the Regent's Park close to the house. Musically, too, he consecrated the album by a composition, the well-known Cradle Song in B flat, written for the occasion.[1]

In the course of years the pages of the little book have been covered with souvenirs from the pens and pencils of such friends as were not unworthy of inscribing their names next to that of the "genius" godfather; it is doubly valued by its possessor, for the interesting autographs it contains, and for the pleasant echoes of the past which it awakens.

On the occasion of a visit to the Portsmouth Dockyard, Mendelssohn's father met with an accident, injuring his leg, and at first there seemed some cause for anxiety. This, however, was soon

[1] See Illustrations, Nos. 15, 16, and 8, respectively.

removed, and nothing but patience was required to insure complete recovery. Much music too must have been prescribed, for we find Mendelssohn and Moscheles constantly at the piano in the patient's room. Amongst other works a collection of Johann Sebastian Bach's Fugues, which Mendelssohn had brought with him, was perused and studied with the greatest interest.

The note upon the next page accompanied a certain Fugue which Mendelssohn had copied out for Moscheles; he is supposed to hold the pen for some of the inmates of the Zoological Gardens, which he and Moscheles had visited in the afternoon.

On one occasion he sent the humorous invitation we reproduce.[1] On another occasion he insisted on having a regular card of invitation, which he filled in as given in our illustration.[2]

Notwithstanding the numerous calls upon his time, Mendelssohn found leisure to make a pianoforte duet arrangement of Moscheles's Septet. Speaking of this in a subsequent letter, Moscheles says: "I have recopied your arrangement of my Septet, and treated several passages more freely than you, with your usual discretion, had done; at the same time I have taken your hint, and added twelve new bars in the first part and altered two towards the end."

Of the many notes that passed between Great Portland Street and Chester Place, we transcribe a few.

[1] See Illustration, No. 12. [2] See Illustration, No. 13.

Zoological Gardens
Aug. 9
1833

Sir! Sir! Sir!

You wou-ou-ou-ld have a copy of this Fu-u-gue, he-eeere we copied it out for youououououaaaou!

Yooour obed[t]. Servants

The grisly Bear;
The Lion
The Wapiti Deer
and
Several young monkies.

9. Fac-simile of Note from the Zoölogical Gardens. (See page 70.)

DEAR MRS. MOSCHELES, —

BOOK I. — ON HEALTH.

I trust you are quite well, even better than you were last night. My father is well, and I have slept nine hours and am tired.

BOOK II. — ON SHOPPING.

My father requests you to let him come to-day or to-morrow morning, to arrange when he may go out with you, according to your kind promise and Stone's prescription (to walk). This note is business-like; you must give me a verbal answer to Book I.

Yours, F. M.

103 GREAT PORTLAND STREET, June 20, 1833.

DEAR MRS. MOSCHELES, — I am very sorry I could not be with you yesterday evening, all the more as I am sure you again thought you had read in my face that I had made up my mind not to go. This time it was not so, however; but the check-taker would on no account let me pass without a ticket. I gave your name; he could not fetch you. I beckoned and called, and as I could not catch your eye, I waited and thought you might pass in my direction; but the cruel Cerberus in livery intimated to me that I had better retire to Portland Street, and that is what I did. . . .

In another note he says: —

Here is my verbal answer — Oh dear! how unlucky, we can't come! You see, we are giving a dinner ourselves to-day. I have just ordered fish and lobster for five, — that is, salmon, — and so I must present our regrets.

103 Great Portland Street, July 17, 1833.

With best thanks I return the books you lent me, namely, Nathan, two volumes of Zschokke, the last volume of "Phantasie-Stücke," and the musical paper; so please destroy whatever acknowledgment of these you may have. Please give bearer the address of that faithless laundress, with whom I should be in a rage if she were not under your immediate patronage.

Best love to Moscheles.

Felix Mendelssohn Bartholdy.

P. S. So far I have not yet learned to tie that cravat (I practised yesterday before the looking-glass); but it is beautiful all the same.

On the 29th of August Mendelssohn left London; and after a short stay in Berlin, he proceeded to Düsseldorf to assume his new duties as "Musik-director." He had accepted this position for three years, at a salary of six hundred thalers per annum, with three months' leave of absence.

The original score of his Overture to the "Isles of Fingal" he gave to Moscheles. We reproduce

At the Residence of Heincke Esqr.

under the immediate Patronage of

several articles of Ironmongery of Distinction

a Grand Miss

Cellaneous Concert

in the splendid Picture Gallery will be

given on the first showery day viz

to-morrow.

Act. I

Conversazione German and English in which will be

introduced several blunders & some French

Mr. Despallers celebrated Song on blue paper,

called for and not sung by Mrs. Moscheles, but

by the whole of the German Chorussesses.

The Duet

as performed with unbounded applause

adjourned at 5 o Clock

to ~~be~~ sit again to-morrow in Committee

August 1833

6.45 P.M.

10. Fac-simile of Humorous Note. (See page 70.)

the first page of it. On perusing it some fifty years after it was written, Gounod made the note at the foot.[1]

SEPT. 13, 1833.

DEAR MRS. MOSCHELES, — Here is Berlin, September 13, and my father once more safely lodged in the Leipzigerstrasse, and feeling quite well. I should write you a long and detailed letter, if I did not wish to send a few words without delay from this place, which we reached yesterday, and which I must leave again the day after to-morrow; you can fancy how the whole day is spent in the family circle, with neither time nor inclination for letter-writing. But to look back upon the anxious days I have gone through, to remember all the kindness shown me, to feel that I am relieved of a great responsibility, and to think of those who assisted me in bearing its weight, — *that* I have both leisure and inclination to do, and that is the purport of this letter. Here all are well and cheerful, and send their best love. My father was unlucky enough to tread a nail into his foot, as we were visiting my uncle's place on the Rhine, on the very day the steamer brought us the Dirichlets.[2] So he was laid up again for several days, and had to perform the whole journey to Berlin stretched out in the coupé. This little accident caused him more depression than his serious

[1] See Illustration, No. 14.

[2] The Dirichlets were his younger sister and her husband, a professor of mathematics.

illness in London, so that he felt excessively impatient to see his own home again, and almost despaired of it. This, and in particular our necessarily slow progress, with so many inns and nights' lodgings, made the whole journey most irksome, and my own impatience became the greater for having to conceal it. But at last I felt happy indeed, as we drove into the well-known courtyard, and the journey was safely over. The foot was but slightly injured, and to-day my father is allowed to walk about.

Excuse haste. I shall write properly from Düsseldorf, where I must be in a few days. And now farewell to you both. My love to Felix, Emily, and Serena. Wish I could send her two carnations. Pray give them to her in my name.

Wishing you all happiness, I am yours,

FELIX MENDELSSOHN BARTHOLDY.

DÜSSELDORF, Nov. 25, 1833.

DEAR MRS. MOSCHELES, — Should this piece of paper have turned red by the time Klingemann arrives, it will but reflect my blushes. But when once a man has become callous, he is no longer amenable to kindness and friendliness; callous he remains, and keeps on sinning to his heart's content. And that, I am sorry to say, is my case. And this does not even pretend to be the answer to your most kind letter, but my own act of accusation, bearing witness that I really received your letter, and nevertheless remained deaf and dumb,

On Mr. Felix Mendelssohn Bartholdy's

REQUEST THE PLEASURE OF

having a printed card has been done to him by Mrs. Moscheles, and as he prefers music and Mrs. Moscheles'

COMPANY TO TEA & CARDS

he has the

honour to accept Mrs. Moscheles'

kind invitation

An answer will oblige him by no means, as he could receive it only in case, the party should be postponed. He hopes, the card, Sold by H Richards 26 G^t Portland S^t, as it was, will be excused by Mrs. Moscheles

II. Card of Invitation filled in by Mendelssohn. (See page 70.)

and that you would be quite justified in not even reading all this. The truth is, that since I have got used to this place, I feel quite at home and settled in it. I am working a good deal for myself and for the outer world, and that, in other words, means that I am happy. This I ought to have described to you at full length, but could not (perhaps Klingemann can do so verbally), and so kept silent; but towards Christmas I mean to send you some new compositions and a letter as well, and then Moscheles must give me his opinion of the music, according to his promise. He will by that time have conducted my Overture in F, and will report about it, so that I shall have a letter in spite of my sins. Now, that is being hardened indeed! Better change the subject.

Herewith is the book of Songs formally made over to you, your heirs, executors, and assigns; if Klingemann does n't give it up, he is worse than a *gazzo-ladro*. I do intend sending you a proper book of manuscript songs at Christmas; but you won't believe me, so I 'll set about writing it first.

And how about Moscheles's four-hand Sonata?

After all, this is but a note, and I ought to conclude by saying: "I am truly sorry I cannot dine with you this day week, because I have a previous engagement at Mrs. Anderson's."

All love to Emily and Serena, and every good wish for your welfare. Should little Felix show his content by saying "Ba!" or otherwise prove his friendly disposition, you must tell him about his godfather, and give him his love. Now farewell, and fare ever well.

Yours,

FELIX MENDELSSOHN BARTHOLDY.

DÜSSELDORF, Feb. 7, 1834.

MY DEAR FRIEND, — Pardon my long silence; I know how guilty I am, but I reckon on your indulgence. I am so deeply buried in my work and papers, that even now I think I should not have emerged from them, were it not that a special circumstance obliges me to write to you. So let me pass over the last four months and all my excuses into the bargain, remembering what a dear old friend you are, and how ready to forgive.

Thus encouraged, I fancy myself in Chester Place, and wish you "Good-evening." What I have to say is this: I have ventured to dedicate to you, without asking your permission, a piece which is to appear at Simrock's, and which I am very fond of. But that is not what I was going to say. I had thought how nice it would be if you met with it during one of your trips to Germany; but now my Rondo Brillant is just finished, and I have the very greatest desire to dedicate that also to you: but I do not venture to do it without your special permission, for I am well aware that it is not the correct thing to ask leave to dedicate two pieces at once; and perhaps you will think it rather an odd proceeding on my part, but I cannot help it, I have set my mind upon it.

First Page of the Original Score of Mendelssohn's Overture to the "Isles of Fingal," given to Moscheles. On perusing it fifty years later, Gounod made the note appended. (See page 77.)

In general, I am not very partial to dedications, and have seldom made any; but in this case they are to convey a meaning, inasmuch as, not having been able to send you a letter for a long while, I wanted at least to let you have some of the work I have been doing. Write me a line on the subject, as the Rondo is to appear in Leipzig too; and once you have written that line you may feel inclined to add another, or perhaps a few more, as you did in your last kind letter, for which I have not even thanked you yet.

Klingemann is not prodigal of words, so that I have heard but little of London friends, and particularly little of those in Chester Place. What do you all look like? What can Felix say? Does Serena remember her humble servant with the carnations? And how fares the Sonata for four hands? Do tell me all about that and your other work. I would ask Mrs. Moscheles to let me know all about it, but I feel she must be so angry with me that I don't think I can summon courage to write to her. The last of your compositions I heard of was the Impromptu for Mary Alexander, and since then I am sure you have produced all manner of delightful things. My own poverty in shaping new forms for the pianoforte once more struck me most forcibly whilst writing the Rondo. It is there I get into difficulties and have to toil and labor, and I am afraid you will notice that such was the case. Still, there are things in it which I believe are not bad, and some parts that I really like; but how I am to set about writing a calm and quiet piece (as you advised me last spring), I really do not know. All that passes through my head in the shape of pianoforte music is about as calm and quiet as Cheapside; and when I sit down to the piano and compel myself to start improvising ever so quietly, it is of no use, — by degrees I fall back into the old ways.

My new Scena,[1] however, which I am writing for the Philharmonic, will, I am afraid, be only too tame. But so much self-criticism is no good; so I stick to my work, and that means, in plain language, that I am well and happy.

I feel particularly comfortable in this place, having just as much official occupation as I want and like, and plenty of time to myself. When I do not feel inclined to compose, there is the conducting and rehearsing, and it is quite a pleasure to see how well and brightly things go; and then the place is so charmingly diminutive that you can always fancy yourself in your own room; and yet it is complete in its way. There is an opera, a choral society, an orchestra, church music, a public, and even a small opposition; it is simply delightful. I have joined a society formed for the improvement of our stage, and we are now rehearsing the "Wasserträger." It is quite touching to see with what eagerness and appetite the singers pounce upon every hint, and what trouble

[1] "Infelice."

they will take if anybody will be at the pains of teaching them; how they strain every nerve and really make our performances as perfect as can be imagined considering the means at our disposal. Last December I gave "Don Juan" (it was the first time I conducted an opera in public), and I can assure you many things went better and with more precision than I have heard them at some of the large and famous theatres, because from first to last every one concerned went in for it heart and soul; well, we had twenty rehearsals. The lessee of the theatre had, however, thought fit to raise the prices on account of the heavy expenses; and when, at the first performance of "Don Juan," the curtain rose, the malcontent section of the public called for Signor Derossi like mad, and made a tremendous disturbance; after five minutes, order was restored, we began and went through the first act splendidly, constantly accompanied by applause; but lo and behold! as the curtain rises for the second act, the uproar breaks out afresh, with redoubled vigor and persistence. Well, I felt inclined to hand the whole concern over to the devil, — never did I conduct under such trying circumstances. I countermanded the opera which was announced for the next night, and declared I would have nothing more to do with the whole theatre; four days later I allowed myself to be talked over, gave a second performance of "Don Juan," was received with hurrahs and a threefold flourish of trumpets, and now the

"Wasserträger" is to follow. The opposition consists mainly of beerhouse keepers and waiters; in fact, by four o'clock P. M., half Düsseldorf is intoxicated. Anybody wanting to see me must call between eight and nine in the morning; it is quite useless attempting to do any kind of business in the afternoon.

Now, what do you think of such a discreditable state of things, and can you have anything more to say to such boors as we are?

By the by, Mr. Spring of Moscow is quite destroying my peace of mind. He would have it that he knew you very well, and I would not believe him on any account; at last he showed me a manuscript note of invitation from Chester Place, and I had to give in, but still I cannot digest him; — a pity that at his age, and with as little talent as he seems to have, he should be obliged to give concerts and make money.

Blagrove was here. I took him to our Choral Society, where we were just rehearsing the choruses from "Alexander's Feast;" our performance produced the most excellent effect on him, — it sent him to sleep.

Can you not send me one or the other of your new things (a copy or whatever you like)? The gentleman who takes charge of this returns shortly, and would, I am sure, be the bearer of your parcel. So, if you have anything, please send it to Klingemann's, and it shall be called for.

I hear from my mother that the "Gipsies'

March," or rather the "April Variations," are out. Is that the case; and if so, could I have a copy of them? I hope you have done a good deal of patching and polishing to my part, — you know, I am thinking of those restless passages of mine. The whole of the last number wants repairing or lining with a warm melody; it was too thin. The first variation, too, I hope you have turned inside out and padded. Don't I speak as if I were Musikdirector Schneider? And can't you send me one of Mori's annual gems? But I must really take courage and another little sheet of paper and write to your wife, for I have n't half done. Good-by — till we meet on the next page.

Your

F. MENDELSSOHN.

DÜSSELDORF, Feb. 7, 1834.

DEAR MRS. MOSCHELES, — It is only after having given two hours to writing to Moscheles, that I venture on the letter to you. Never have I so richly deserved a scolding as now; I say deserved, for I may not get it, you have so often let me off. What, as compared with my other delinquencies, are such trifling peccadilloes as talking German at dinner, not carving at the Stones', having threadbare coat-buttons, and not paying compliments *à la* Hummel? But does it perhaps give you satisfaction to hear that I have a very bad conscience, or that I have some kind of feeling like a naughty child about to confess, or that Klingemann too has given up writing to me? To speak seriously, there are many minutes in the course of each day when I think of your dear home, wishing I were there, and enjoying the recollections of the time I have spent in it. That much you must believe; but whether out of such thoughts grows a letter or not, depends more or less upon chance. I am sorry to say I shall not be going to England this spring. I mean to have a good spell of work, and have something to show for it before I stir from here. You can hardly imagine how much better and brighter I feel for the last two months' work, and how much easier I get on with it; so I must keep it up, and get into full swing. My birthday just came in time to remind me how necessary this was. Of my life here, I have already written a good deal to Moscheles. The other day we gave "Egmont" with Beethoven's music. I doubly enjoyed it, for I had n't heard anything of his for a long time.

By the by, you are rather opposed to Goethe in some things; so I recommend you to read a newly published correspondence between him and Zelter, in which you will find plenty of matter to confirm your opinion; and yet I should vigorously oppose you, and stand up for my old favorite as formerly. Do you know the chorus on Lord Byron, which occurs in the second part of "Faust" and begins with "Nicht allein"? Should you not know it, pray read it at once, for I believe it will please

13. Chester Place. From a Drawing made by Mendelssohn in an autograph album given by him to his godchild.
(See page 69.)

you. Just now English tea-time is coming on, and with it I feel all my fear vanishing. To-day there is a *grand déjeuner dansant,* — of all the hateful Berlin institutions the one I hate the most. A nice set they are! They meet at half-past eleven A. M., and spend their time eating and drinking until one o'clock next morning. There are few things so unsightly in my eyes, whether it is done in broad daylight, which is one way; or whether the shutters are closed at midday, and the chandeliers lighted, as they do at Court in Berlin. Besides, there has been dancing for the last fortnight, usually up to five o'clock in the morning, with Prince Frederick taking the lead, giving as many balls and accepting as many invitations as possible. I have been saved all these splendors by a bad cold, which has confined me to my room for more than a week. I am getting over it now; but it will serve as an excuse for keeping aloof until the end of the Carnival. So you see that we too are metropolitan to the best of our abilities; and if this page of mine has not made you feel quite Berlinese or Bœotian, an account of all our dinner-parties, I am sure, would.

I wanted to send you some new songs, but must again put it off, as I have a great deal to prepare for this parcel. I should like to know, too, how you are getting on with your singing, — whether you practise sometimes, and follow the wise rules of your wise professor.[1] You want to know

[1] Meaning himself.

whether I am rapidly degenerating here, and whether I stand in awe of any one as I did of you with regard to elegance, or rather neatness? Madame Hübner, whom you must have seen at Berlin, does sometimes take me to task, and sees at a glance, on my entering a room, some shortcoming which it might take me six months to notice; but she is not as good a Mentor as you, so that I fear you will find me quite run wild, should I venture again out of my backwoods; and as for my capacity for tying a cravat with taste, that will be a thing of the past. But when we meet, you will find me as willing a pupil as ever.

Love to Emily and Serena and to my little godson. The little man cannot yet understand it, but never mind. Adieu then, and be well and happy.

Ever your

FELIX MENDELSSOHN BARTHOLDY.

On the 12th of February, 1834, Moscheles writes:—

I have read and studied your Overture ("Melusine") with ever-growing interest; and let me say, in the fewest of words, that it is a splendid work. It is marked by vigorous and spirited conception, unity, and originality. Thus impressed, I proceeded to the first rehearsal, after having gone through it privately with Mori. But it was not an easy matter to moderate the orchestra in the *piano* parts; especially at the outset they would make a desperate plunge, and the trumpets were somewhat surprised at having to fall in with their 7th on C. I winced and groaned, and made them begin again three times. The contrasting storms went as if Neptune held the sceptre; but when the voices of the Sirens were to disarm that boisterous ruler, I had to call for *piano, piano! piano!* at the top of my voice, bending down to the ground, *à la* Beethoven,[1] and in vain trying to restrain the ferocious violins and basses. However, at a second reading things went better. The work was studied with the liveliest interest, and received with the fullest appreciation. I hope to bring out the lights and shades still better at the performance. You have given the horns and trumpets, alternately, the

which they rendered splendidly with stopping and damping.

After yours I had Berlioz's Overture, "Les Francs Juges," to conduct. We were all curious to know what the result of French genius would be. I say French, for so far no other country but France has recognized Berlioz as a genius. But, oh! what a rattling of brass, fit for the Porte Saint-Martin! What cruel, wicked scoring! as if to prove that our ancestors were no better than

[1] Alluding to Beethoven's habit, in conducting, of crouching down at a *pianissimo* and flying up at a *forte*.

pedants! And, oh! again, for the contrast of the middle subject, that would console us with a vaudeville melody, such as you could not hear to more advantage in "L'Ours et le Pacha," or the "Viennese in Berlin." Then the mystic element, — a progression of screeching harmonies, unintelligible to all but the March cats! To show that something terrible is agitating the fevered brain of the composer, an apoplectic stroke of the big drum shakes to shivers the efforts of the whole orchestra, as also the auditory nerves of the assembled audience. . . .

Our "Gipsies' March" is out, — in London at Cramer's, in Paris at Schlesinger's, in Leipzig at Kistner's. Kistner has sent a copy in our name to Frau von Goethe, to whom we have dedicated the piece. You approve of that dedication to her, don't you? Your half-share of the proceeds is, eight Napoleons from Schlesinger, eight Louis d'or from Kistner, and fifteen to twenty pounds from Cramer.

I will carefully keep the account; so, if you want money, draw on your banker and friend,

I. MOSCHELES.

DÜSSELDORF, April, 1834.

MY DEAR MOSCHELES, — I cannot tell you how much pleasure those letters from you and from your wife gave me. I don't think the post ever put me in such high spirits before. I certainly never felt so happy and elated for days together

14. Regent's Park. From a Sketch made by Mendelssohn in an autograph album given by him to his godchild (See page 69.)

as I did after getting them. You know how often I am beset by grievous misgivings, how I cannot do anything to my satisfaction, and how, when such doubts lay hold of me, I fancy the whole world must be aware of my shortcomings, even more than I am myself, and must overlook the very existence of my works. But such kind and friendly words as you have written about my Overture give me greater pleasure than anything that I could hear after completing a composition. This I know for a certainty: you might have sent me three of the finest Russian orders or titles for the Overture without giving me one hour's happiness such as I have had from your letter. Do you really know how kind and amiable you were? Because, if you do, I need not attempt to thank you.

But now let me say how grateful I am for all the trouble you have taken with my Overture. It is quite a painful feeling to have a piece performed and not to be present, not to know what succeeded and what went wrong; but when *you* are conducting I really feel less nervous than if I were there myself, for no one can take more interest in his own works than you do in those of others, and then you can hear and take note of a hundred things that the composer, preoccupied as he is, has no time or mind for.

I had already heard from Klingemann what a true friend you had been to my Overture, and now your description puts it all so visibly before me. After reading your letter, I took up the score, and played it straight through from beginning to end, and felt that I liked it better than before.

By the way, you complain of the difficulty in getting the *pianos* observed; and as I was playing the piece over again, it struck me that that was really my fault. It is easily remedied, for the whole thing, I believe, is due to the marks of expression; if you have those altered in the parts, it will be set right at once. First, everything should be marked one degree weaker; that is, where there is a *p* in the wind instruments, it should be *pp;* instead of *mf*, *piano;* instead of *f*, *mf*. The *pp* alone might remain, as I particularly dislike *ppp*. The *sf*'s, however, should be everywhere struck out, as they really are quite wrong, no abrupt accent being meant, but a gradual swelling of the tone, which is sufficiently indicated by the <. The same again wherever the

etc. recurs; in all such passages the *sf*'s should be done away with; and in the strings as well: for instance, at the very opening, and where the trumpets first come in, it should be *pp;* the *f*'s should simply disappear. Klingemann would, I am sure, oblige me by making these alterations in the score, a copyist would transfer them to the parts, and then the whole thing would sound twice as mermaidish.

What you say of Berlioz's Overture I thoroughly agree with. It is a chaotic, prosaic piece, and yet more humanly conceived than some of his others. I always felt inclined to say with Faust, —

> "He ran around, he ran about,
> His thirst in puddles laving;
> He gnawed and scratched the house throughout,
> But nothing cured his raving;
> And driven at last, in open day,
> He ran into the kitchen."

For his orchestration is such a frightful muddle, such an incongruous mess, that one ought to wash one's hands after handling one of his scores. Besides, it really is a shame to set nothing but murder, misery, and wailing to music; even if it were well done, it would simply give us a record of atrocities. At first he made me quite melancholy, because his judgments on others are so clever, so cool, and correct, he seems so thoroughly sensible, and yet he does not perceive that his own works are such rubbishy nonsense. I am very glad to hear what you say about the "Gipsy Variations;" but do tell me whether you are not treating me much too liberally, for I never in my life should have dreamed of such high terms as now fall to my share alone. The E flat for the horns and trumpets I put down trusting to luck, and hoping that Providence would show the players some way to do it; if they have new contrivances for it, so much the better.

You sent me word not to let Mori have anything more gratis, on account of his indiscretion; I am doubly sorry for this, as I have just presented him with a manuscript, to make up for having kept him waiting six months for the Rondo. I did not like the idea of his having to pardon any shortcoming of mine, so I thought it the best way out of the difficulty, and now, although regretting the circumstance, I must of course keep my word; but for the future I will act upon your hint. That piece for Fanny Stone I should of all things like to write, but how am I to compose something easy? Well, I will set about it, and do my best to avoid octaves and broken chords; then there will be no ornamental passages at all, for you know I never write any others. No, but really I will look out seriously for a piece that I can dedicate to her.

But now I must write a few lines to your wife and beg her soon to let me have more of such good news about my dear Master Felix and Miss Serena and the grown-up young lady.

I suppress my thanks to you, dear Mrs. Moscheles, for all the kind things you say; I only wish I could now and then write something which would give you real pleasure, and that I could believe myself worthy of doing so.

I have just had a letter from my sister in Berlin. She tells me you had written all about the Overture to my father, and had given him immense pleasure; and there again I must particularly thank you, for you know how pleasant it is to have one's praises sung to one's parents.

I do wish I could once more call Emily "Du," but this spring I shan't be able to get away; in fact, I shall probably not travel at all, but buy a horse, and ride and swim and work all through the summer. Next spring, when, please God, I once more knock at the door of No. 3 Chester Place, I shall speak English and say, "You;" that will appear less strange to me than the formal "Sie." Then, when I return some day a long time hence, I shall sit and play at *écarté* whilst she dances, and shall notice Mr. Stone or some other young man extremely attentive to her. To be sure, he will have to be very cautious about it, for fear of losing your good graces. And then Felix will show me the score of his first Symphony and play it with Serena. By that time I shall be a *vieux garçon* or a *ci-devant jeune homme*, — but this is n't a pleasant subject; better drop it; it was really you who put me on to it by your artful allusions to the better things awaiting me, and by your remarks about the *soirée* at the Taylors', and about Mrs. Handley, who, by the side of her husband, must look like a white mouse by the side of a black tom-cat, or like a duet for clarinet and double bassoon, or kid gloves and a Warsaw dressing-gown, or vanilla ice next to roast beef, etc. You see at a glance that I am still a warm admirer of hers, or I should not compare her to such nice things, but rather to Maraschino ice, or a hautboy. I returned last night from a trip to Cologne, where I had to play at a charity concert, and where your description of the Cologne public and Cologne musicians, so dear to you, was most vividly brought back to my mind. I would rather live in any village than there; and much as I like Düsseldorf, I do not believe I could live for even a couple of months at Cologne.

I am taking regular lessons in water-colors now with one of our artists, and work most enthusiastically for several hours every Sunday morning. Shall I send you a sketch? And what country is it to represent? Switzerland or Italy? In the foreground I shall introduce a girl with a green apron and a carnation, to ingratiate myself with Serena. I only wish I had more leisure, but just now all my time is taken up by the rehearsals of the "Wasserträger."

By the by, do you know a book by Thomas Moore[1] on religion? It has lately appeared; it is said to have gone through at least seventy editions, and to extinguish all Protestants, Dissenters, nations, and nationality. It is read here by all the Orthodox Catholics, and praised highly.

I have lately read Shakspeare's "King John" for the first time. I do assure you it is downright heavenly, like everything else of his. But now I must end at once, or I shall begin talking about Goethe and Zelter's letters, which I did not like

[1] Travels of an Irish Gentleman in Search of a Religion.

much. You are of a different opinion, so my letter might become not only long, but tedious, which it is already; besides, the paper obliges me to conclude. Should Emily or Serena ask after me, or the baby be in good humor and crow, and should that American prodigy be so completely "finished" that not one finger remains untrained, or should some lady — thank Heaven — put off her lesson or not come, then, and that as soon as possible, let me have a few lines telling me that Chester Place is flourishing.

Once more thanks, and farewell.

FELIX M. B.

DÜSSELDORF, May 11, 1834.

DEAR MRS. MOSCHELES, — On the very day I received your dear kind letter and the beautiful present, I was going to answer at full length, and with best thanks, but there arrived at the same time the news of my mother's dangerous illness. To-day there is excellent news, thank God! My mother has been walking in the garden, and is quite herself, and of course so am I; and in this happy mood, when a great load has been taken off my mind, and I can breathe more freely, I sit down at once to write and thank you.

Not being able to cross over to you this year, I do hope and trust you will let me have a few lines now and then; for while I read them I am in Chester Place, I follow your descriptions, live through it all with you, rejoice at Lord Burghersh's absence from the party, make remarks about Miss Masson's delicate form of "couching her refusal," abuse Masoni for that Beethoven Sonata, and admire Miss Use's beauty, although I know it only by hearsay.

And how grateful I am to you, dear Moscheles, for doing my Rondo the honor of playing it at your concert! You may believe that I fully appreciate it, and feel greatly flattered; and now, if anybody abuses it ever so much, I shall still love the piece and hold it in high consideration. Please write me word if you like the accompaniments, or if you find fault with any part of them. I may perhaps write something of the kind in the course of this year, and should like to avoid former faults.

The cravat, however, dear Mrs. Moscheles, I put on at once, and, so adorned, went out for a ride. You must know I have bought a nice bay horse, and it gives me immense pleasure. When I went to the Hübners' in the evening, Madame Hübner asked if that cravat was English too. I gave her your message, and she reciprocated it very sincerely. But you have not told me what composition I am to write in the time saved by this cravat which does not require tying. It is to you I shall owe the spare time, and you ought to say how I am to employ it. Shall I write pianoforte pieces, songs, or what else?

And so the people at the Philharmonic did not like my "Melusine"? Never mind; that won't kill me. I felt sorry when you told me, and at once played the Overture through, to see if I too should dislike it; but it pleased me, and so there is no great harm done. Or do you think it would make you receive me less amiably at my next visit? That would be a pity, and I should much regret it; but I hope it won't be the case. And perhaps it will be liked somewhere else, or I can write another one which will have more success. The first desideratum is to see a thing take shape and form on paper; and if, besides, I am fortunate enough to get such kind words about it as those I had from you and Moscheles, it *has* been well received, and I may go on quietly doing more work. I cannot understand your news that Moscheles's new Concerto met with the same reception. I thought it as clear as sunshine that *that* must please the public, when played by him. But when is it to be published, that I may pounce upon it? Pray do excuse these disconnected sentences. Ries, the violin-player, is here (you remember his playing in Moscheles's Trio at Berlin); he is going to give a concert to-morrow, and so I have been constantly interrupted by all sorts of people employed in the arrangements, and have to rehearse every day, in consequence of which my poor bay has not left its stable for the last three days (this, you see, is the principal subject on which my mind turns).

At Whitsuntide I must go to Aix-la-Chapelle to the musical festival, and am not the least inclined for it, since they perform pieces which my musical conscience revolts at; but go I must, for a quiet life, as the people of this place will have it that Ries and I are pope and anti-pope; and, Ries happening to conduct, they fancy me jaundiced with vexation, and think that I shall not go. But they are mistaken; I sip my "Maitrank," — an excellent drink made of hock, aromatic herbs, and sugar, — and mean to go. This reminds me of Siboni. Oh, Siboni! how can you presume seriously to bring out your recipes for salad-mixing? And is De Vrught there too? And what sort of a figure does he cut at a dinner in Chester Place? Stop! By the by, have you heard of a Mademoiselle Meyer who has gone with her father from here to London to play the piano? She must, some time or other, pass in review before Moscheles, and I should like above all things to hear of her doings in London. The father *would* set me up here as his daughter's rival, and has tried to abuse and vex me in every way, and, finding that I took no notice, is going to try what he can do in London.

Lovely weather we have had for some time, and there is every temptation to be perfectly idle, saunter about all day, and become a candidate for the title of Inspector of Nightingales, which they have conferred on an old lounger of this place. Warm days, and so delightfully long, and I have already begun my Oratorio, which is the reason I cannot go to the Westminster Abbey Festival, but must keep to my work. I have writ-

15. "Maillied," in Letter of May 15, 1834, to Mrs. Moscheles. (See page 107.)

ten a few Capriccios for the pianoforte (or Fantasias, or ——) that I like very well, but an abominable *Étude*. This morning, for the first time after a long interval, a song has come to me; and such a present is at all times refreshing. I really must write it down for you, although I am sorry to say it is not at all suited for your voice, but rather for a tenor. You need not even play it; yet I write it down for you all the same. Moscheles can hum the melody to himself.

MAILIED.

sf
lein. Du zar - tes Jung-fräu-lein, Du bist mein Au - - - gen -
sf
p
schein, Du bist mein Au-gen - schein. Wär ich bei Dir al -
p
pp
sf espres.
lein ! Kein Leid sollt mich anfechten, Wollt' all-zeit
sf
sf p

Dein Reiz ist aus der Maassen
Gleichwie der Pfauen Art,
Wenn Du gehst auf der Strassen,
Gar oft ich Deiner wart',
Gar oft ich Deiner wart'.
Ob ich gleich viel muss stehn

Im Regen und im Schnee,
Im Regen und im Schnee,
Kein Müh soll mich verdriessen,
Wenn ich Dich Herzlieb seh',
Wenn ich Dich Herzlieb seh',
Wenn ich Dich Herzlieb seh'.

(Aus dem Wunderhorn.)

MAY 14.

This letter was begun three days ago, and I have not yet been able to finish it. Ries has left again. We played Beethoven's grand Sonata in A minor, dedicated to Kreutzer, at his concert, and that by heart, which was great fun. I do not know whether I told Moscheles that the scores of my three overtures, "Midsummer Night's Dream," "Meeresstille," and "Isles of Fingal," will appear in a few days at Breitkopf & Härtel's, which makes me unspeakably proud. As soon as they are to be had, they shall be presented to you, and I only wish I could have again dedicated them to you, my dear Moscheles; but as that would n't do, my friends at home wished me to inscribe them to the Crown Prince, who has shown himself extremely gracious to me this last autumn. For my own part, I was thinking of the Philharmonic, and so it is undecided. A knotty point, you see.

And do you know, dear Mrs. Moscheles, that Varnhagen is going to be married again, — six months after his inconsolable book about his wife, — and that to my cousin Marianna Saaling. A young musician has just been here with an atrocious Fugue for me to look through; also another native genius who feels an impulse to write Chorales, enough to make one turn yellow with impatience; and yet he has written Chorales ever since I came here, the last always worse than the one before it; and as we go on being vexed with one another, there are some lovely scenes, he not being able to understand that I still find his compositions bad, and I that he has not improved them. I am, however, the very type of a good Cantor, and preach so much to the point that it is great fun to hear me. The lilies of the valley are out; how pleased I should be to send Serena some! But even without them, may she live and prosper, and Emily and Felix as well. And how about Emily's tune? Now there is an end to my paper; indeed, I have talked nonsense enough.

Ever yours,

FELIX MENDELSSOHN BARTHOLDY.

DÜSSELDORF, June 26, 1834.

YOU AMIABLE COUPLE IN CHESTER PLACE!—Let me thank you a thousand times for that nice, good, kind letter that you have treated me to again; they are high days and holidays for me when I receive your letters, and can read them over and over again. If you, my dear Moscheles, thank me for the Rondo, I must thank you for thanking me; but I still maintain you are too indulgent. The other day, Dr. Frank, whom you know, came to Düsseldorf, and I wished to show him something of my A major Symphony. Not having it here, I began writing out the Andante again, and in so doing I came across so many *errata* that I got interested and wrote out the Minuet and Finale too, but with many necessary alterations; and whenever such occurred I thought of you, and of how you never said a word of blame, although you must have seen it all much better and plainer than I do now. The first movement I have not written down, because, if once I begin with that, I am afraid I shall have to alter the entire subject, beginning with the fourth bar,—

and that means pretty nearly the whole first piece, — and I have no time for that just now. The dominant in the fourth bar strikes me as quite disagreeable; I think it should be the seventh (A–G). But many thanks to you and the Philharmonic for playing so much of my music. I am sure I am delighted, if only the public does not grumble!

And what do you say to their hissing little Herz? Why, that implies a high degree of culture! Has he consoled himself with guineas and pupils, or was it too crushing? You are particularly silent on the subject; and yet it is true, and Moritz Schlesinger will not be slow to triumph. Well, if he will only abstain from writing Variations for four hands, or, if that is too much to ask, if he will only avoid winding up with those Rondos that are so frightfully vulgar that I am ashamed to play them to decent people, then, for aught I care, let him be made King of the Belgians, or rather Semiquaver King, just as one says "Fire-King." After all, I like him; he certainly is a characteristic figure of these times, of the year 1834; and as Art should be a mirror reflecting the character of the times, — as Hegel or some one else probably says somewhere, — he certainly does reflect most truly all salons and vanities, and a little yearning, and a deal of yawning, and kid gloves, and musk, a scent I abhor. If in his latter days he should take to the Romantic and write melancholy music, or to the Classical and give us fugues, — and I should not be surprised if he did,—Berlioz can compose a new symphony on him, "De la Vie d'un Artiste," which I am sure will be better than the first.

Stop; by the by, a few hours after my last letter was posted I altered the beginning of my "Wunderhornlied," although I had not noticed the resemblance, and simply because I did not like it; and now comes your remark about the reminiscence, which is very striking. Who in the wide world will believe that I altered it before? You, for one, I hope. Anyhow, there is the date upon it, and the following beginning:—

What do I think of Vrught? I really have heard him too little to judge, — only once, and then he sang a song in two verses: the first quite simply and in his natural voice, so that I thought him the greatest singer I had ever heard, — it was truly beautiful; but in the second verse it was all shakes and skipping about, and I quickly changed my mind. Since then he has not behaved very well to me; but, for my part, I have no objection to giving him a copy of my Scena, only I do not think I can do so on account of the Philharmonic.

There is a passage in your letter, dear Mrs. Moscheles, that I protest I am mightily offended at. You say I declare that your letters are agreeable to me; and *that* I am sure I have never *declared*, because it is simply a fact. Besides, "agreeable" is not the right word: I am really grateful for the pleasure they give me. Then you say, too, I am not to care for public and critics; and that is just as bad. Am I not by trade an anti-public-caring musician, and an anti-critic-caring one into the bargain? What is Hecuba to me, and what the press (I mean the press that depresses)? And if this very day I had an idea for an Overture to Lord Eldon, in the form of a canon *alla rovescia*, or of a double fugue with a *cantus firmus*, write it I would, although I knew it could never become popular; how much more the lovely Melusina, — a very different subject! Only it certainly would be annoying if one never had a chance of hearing one's things performed; but as you say that is not to be feared, let us wish the public and critics long life and happiness, — and me too, — and let me live to go to England next year.

Oh, Seigneur de Fahl, you live in my rooms! If rooms could speak, what stuff they would tell me next year, or what would they have told you! But I hope he is not going to remain in London, for if I could not have my rooms in No. 103 Great Portland Street it would put me out very much, since I lived there through so much of sweet and so much of bitter, — a whole chapter of my life.

Yes, certainly, my horse is more attractive than all the young ladies I knew in Berlin, it is so glossy and brown; then it looks so healthy and so very good-natured (and good-nature, every one knows, is not exactly what the Berlinese are noted for). However, I do not forswear marriage, for my father has prophesied that I shall never marry. There certainly is little hope of it just now, but I shall lose no opportunity of getting myself placed; and surely, if Varnhagen has succeeded twice, why should I not finally meet with some girl who would take me?

From Frau von Goethe I have a very kind letter, in which she sends me so many thanks for the Variations that I feel I ought to forward the greater part of them to you, my dear Moscheles.

Now let me write my message to Serena, and inform her that I shall pay her a visit next year, and present her with a large nosegay of pinks;

and to Emily I will bring a brand-new tune, and teach it to her. Will you have some mustard or an oil picture?—those are the only choice productions of the place. And what am I to do in the mean while with my Choir, and the Opera, and my horse? Well, there 's plenty of time to think of that; so now good-night and *au revoir!*

When Moscheles has a moment of leisure let him send me a line and his best love. No more room to sign my name.

Moscheles gives Mendelssohn full particulars of the Birmingham Festival. An Oratorio of the Chevalier Neukomm's and an unusually large number of the same composer's works figured in the programme. "His style is Haydn's," says Moscheles; "occasionally elevated and bordering on Handel, but when you go into detail, you find many hackneyed modulations and figures. For the higher development of Art he has not done much, but in his 'David' there are numbers showing excellent workmanship and much ability in the use of all the means at his disposal."

A Fantasia on the Organ he entitled "A Concert on a Lake, interrupted by a Thunderstorm." The poetical element was missing, and the introduction of incidental thunderclaps and forked lightning on the organ only served to show up the weakness of construction in the whole thing.

Moscheles goes on to describe with enthusiasm the performance of the "Messiah" and of some of the most effective Choruses selected from "Israel in Egypt." In speaking of the brass instruments, he says that the ophicleide is a very useful addition to the orchestra in large performances; "for," he remarks, "just as you say of a steam-engine, it has ten-horse power, so of this you can say, it has ten-trombone power."

DÜSSELDORF, Dec. 25, 1834.

DEAR MOSCHELES, — Upon my word, I cannot stand my own base ingratitude any longer! I really must write at last. And why have n't I done so for the last two months? I really cannot say, and certainly cannot find an excuse. The monkeys on the Orinoco, I recollect reading somewhere, do not talk because they have nothing to say, and I suppose I was somewhat of their kind; and then really I was at first in no mood for anything and had plenty of time, and then I was in high spirits and had no time at all, — in fact, I procrastinated. And now that I am about it, what in the name of worry am I to write about from Düsseldorf to a Londoner, and to such a one as you? Really this is such a mite of a place, where nothing ever happens. I cannot possibly send you the news that the Tories are in power. Never mind; I write that I may soon again hear from you. It is just because your letters give me so much pleasure, and bring your interesting life so vividly before me, that I would rather say nothing about our petty provincial affairs. Whilst you are driving at headlong speed, we are really driven like a herd of cattle.

I have one fault to find with your letter. But for Klingemann, I should not have known that you had composed an Overture to "Joan of Arc;" yet you surely cannot doubt that that, of all news, would interest me most. I congratulate you with all my heart if only on the choice of such an excellent and serious subject. I long to hear the Overture itself, but you are absolutely silent about it; in fact, I am quite in ignorance of what you have composed lately, or what you have got in your mind. Please give me full particulars of it, — in what key it is, how it is worked out, and how scored. If possible, jot down a few notes for me. And have you written nothing new for the piano? It would be quite a boon, for there is great dearth in that line.

Thanks for your description of the Festival; it is so graphic and interesting that I could have fancied myself there: I hear Neukomm extemporizing, and see Miss Rylands in the box. (Your account and your wife's must be taken together.)

I quite agree with you in all you say about Neukomm's music. Is n't it wonderful that a man of such taste and refinement should not be able to transfer those qualities to his music? To say nothing of the fundamental ideas of his compositions, the working out seems so careless and commonplace. The Fantasia is probably an example of that kind of thing; and had I come as the most favorably predisposed of listeners, the very title would have scared me away. Then, again, that constant use of the brass! As a matter of sheer calculation it should be sparingly employed, let alone the question of Art! That 's where I admire Handel's glorious style; when he brings up his kettledrums and trumpets towards the end, and thumps and batters about to his heart's content, as if he meant to knock you down — no mortal man can remain unmoved. I really believe it is far better to imitate such work, than to overstrain the nerves of your audience, who, after all, will at last get accustomed to Cayenne pepper. There is Cherubini's new Opera, "Ali Baba," for instance, which I have just been looking through. I was delighted with some parts, but in others it grieved me to find him chiming in with that perverted new fad of the Parisians, winding up pieces, in themselves calm and dignified, with thunder-clap effects, scoring as if instruments were nothing and effect everything, three or four trombones blasting away at you as if the human ear could stand anything. Then the finales with their uncouth harmonies, tearing and dashing about, enough to make an end of you. How bright and sparkling, on the other hand, are some of the pieces in his former manner; between Faniska and Lodoiska, for instance, and this there really is as wide a difference as between a man and a scarecrow, — no wonder the Opera was a failure. To an admirer of old Cherubini's it really is annoying that he should write such miserable stuff, and not have the pluck to resist the so-called taste of the day and of the public, (as if you and I were not part of the public, and did n't live in these times as well, and did n't want music adapted to *our* digestive capacities!) As for those who are not admirers of old Cherubini, they will not be satisfied anyhow, do what he may; for them he is too much himself in "Ali Baba," and after the first three notes they spot their man and put him down as a "vieille perruque," "rococo," etc.

You will fancy I am in an all-devouring mood to-day; not at all,—I really don't know what made me so pugnacious; on the contrary, I am in a most happy, peaceful frame of mind. It is Christmas Day; a fragrant odor of black gingerbread, with which I was regaled at the Schadows' last night, pervades the room; all around are presents from home,—a lounging jacket, writing materials, confectionery, cup and saucer, etc. In the midst of such splendors I have been happy and cheerful all day long, and now in the evening that wicked pen of mine runs away with me. Düsseldorf, too, is not half as bad as I described it just now, and you would not be slow to appreciate it if you heard the members of our Choral Society sing their Sebastian Bach, true knights as they are. We are soon going to perform the "Seasons," and during Lent the "Messiah;" in the last concert we had Weber's "Lyre and Sword," the first part of "Judas Maccabæus," and the "Sinfonia Eroica."

I am held in tremendous respect here; but do you know, I think my ink has turned sour just now because my horse bolted with me this afternoon and ran like mad right through our Corso and half the town, straight to the stables. I kept my seat, but I was in such a rage; and were n't the people just delighted to see the "Herr Musikdirector" racing along! And then really there are not enough pretty girls here; after all, one does n't want to be composing fugues and chorales all day long; but, upon my soul, I am getting so frumpy and old-fashioned that I dread the thought of putting on a dress-coat, and how I am to get on if I go to England next spring and have to wear shoes, I know not. Well, it will all come right again if I am really sufficiently advanced with my work in the spring to cross; and if so, you know with what feelings I look forward to No. 3 Chester Place.

My Oratorio is making great progress. I am working at the second part, and have just written a Chorus in F sharp minor (a lively chorus of heathens) which I thoroughly relish myself and should so much like to show you; in fact, I am ever so anxious to hear whether you are satisfied with my new work. I have lately written some Fugues, Songs without words and with words, and a few Studies, and should of all things like to take a new Concerto for piano with me to London, but of that I know nothing as yet. You once said it was time I should write a quiet, sober piece for the pianoforte, after all those restless ones; and that advice is always running in my head and stops me at the outset, for as soon as I think of a pianoforte piece, away I career, and scarcely am I off when I remember, "Moscheles said, etc.," and there 's an end to the piece. But never mind, I 'll get the better of it yet; and if it turns out restless again, it will certainly not be for want of good intentions.

But now good-by, my dear Moscheles. When you have a leisure hour give me good news and much of it. Remain my friend, as I am yours,

FELIX MENDELSSOHN BARTHOLDY.

With the following letter Mendelssohn sent a small, highly finished water-color drawing of the Bridge of Sighs at Venice to Mrs. Moscheles, which we reproduce.

DÜSSELDORF, Jan. 10, 1835.

DEAR MRS. MOSCHELES, — I ought to be kneeling on peas to do penance, all the time I am writing this letter, sinner that I am! And indeed, in my innermost heart, I am really on peas, when I think of my long silence. Such a shocking return for your kind letter after the Birmingham Festival! The courier who is to take my long-promised sketch to you leaves to-morrow, or I should scarcely have written to-day. The fact that I write only to accompany the sketch, you must not look upon as an aggravation of my offence,

16. The Bridge of Sighs. From a Water-Color Drawing by Mendelssohn.
(See page 122.)

but must interpret it favorably. You know, there are times when I feel but a poor mortal, and avoid speaking or even thinking about myself. Such times come upon me every now and then; and having no kind friend here to turn to for sympathy, I suffer more than elsewhere. If just on a day of that kind a letter reaches me like your last, I am carried into the midst of your busy interesting life, and, comparing that with the monotony of my own existence, I feel as if I could not write a word about myself; in such times, to speak of myself and my work, depresses me still more. Then I fancy I am but a nuisance, and don't write to you. So it has been hitherto; but to-day I turn over a new leaf, and must present my water-color drawing to you, which I herewith do most gracefully. My most solemn and impressive bow you must here picture to yourself.

The sketch, taken at Venice in October, 1830, represents the Bridge of Sighs. Should it be out of drawing, you must n't set that down to me, but fancy the Doge's palace just tumbling down, and consequently leaning on one side. The water is the *partie honteuse*. I have labored the whole morning to make it a little clearer, but it only got muddier; so there, again, imagine that the tide happens to be out, because then the water throughout Venice gets thick and muddy, and might look as unattractive as it does in my sketch. My sky, too, is rather murky; but a certain Nicolaï of Berlin has just published a stupid book meant to prove that there is nothing worth looking at in Italy, — that the country is devoid of beauty, and the people dull and heavy, no *Weissbier*, no oranges, and the sky no better than our own. If he speaks the truth, it would make the color of my sky right. Should my drawing, with all its shortcomings, find favor in your eyes, let me know, that I may make you another; for I am improving, and my next will be better; I might paint you a Swiss landscape, with meadows and houses, for nothing amuses me more. And now if I could only carry this one to you myself, and then and there alter it according to your suggestions!

I shall be glad if I can get to you in the spring; though, much as I desire it, I fear it will hardly be possible. I shall have done my work by that time just as I planned it; but the question is, Ought I to begin something fresh, and go on working quietly, or should I take a holiday? However, one thing I do know, and that is, if I treat myself to a visit to England this year, I will lead a very different life in London to what I did before, — trying to keep as quiet and retired as I do here, and not going into society unless really obliged to; but as to you, I shall inundate you with as many visits as you can endure. Till then I must work hard at my piano, for I fear I have lost ground a good deal. The other day, however, in telling a friend how Moscheles and I used to improvise together, and showing him some of the passages,

I could have given anything to start for London, once more to enjoy the same pleasure; for not only do I play but little here myself, but I rarely get to hear others. On the other hand, there are what I call good days, and most enjoyable ones, when the work prospers, and I have a long morning to myself in my own quiet room; then life is charming indeed.

And pray, how do you all get on? Is there already some "miss" playing her scales downstairs in Moscheles's study, or is he allowed a little leisure to compose and make music? Does little Felix cry very much? Has Emily grown? Of her growing up, you know I stand in mortal fear. I was going to send you another song to-day, but could not get on with it, which annoys me; so you must even rest satisfied with this dull, unmusical letter. And now farewell. May you all be happy and merry in this new year! May it bring you every blessing, and to me a happy meeting with you and Moscheles! All my belongings keep sending messages, which I never give you, although my father is always mentioning your kindness to him and his regard for you.

Ever yours,

FELIX MENDELSSOHN BARTHOLDY.

DÜSSELDORF, Feb. 7, 1835.

DEAR MOSCHELES, AND DEAR MRS. MOSCHELES, —I sent you two such stupid letters the other day by the courier that I really must try if I can't put together a more sensible one to-day. I do feel sometimes as if all the world of Philistines had got the better of me, and I were a Philistine myself; at such times I cannot write, as I amply proved the other day.

To-day I composed a chorus for my Oratorio, and I am quite pleased with it. So what better can I do in the evening than put my happy mood into the shape of a letter to Chester Place, and send my best love to you all? I heard too from Klingemann to-day, and that always makes me feel holiday-like; and besides, it was so desperately foggy that I quite fancied myself in England during my ride; and then for the last few weeks the number of Philistines sitting on me has decreased; and then — and then — spring is coming, and spring weather has come already — so, after all, life is worth living. By the way, is there a word in English for *Philister?* I don't believe there is. Oh, land of happiness!

True, they may re-elect Mr. Fleming to a seat in Parliament; they may sing "Lord God of Israel" to my "Ave," which is much as if they sang "The Old English Gentleman" to Lutzow's "Jagd;" but for all that they are not really Philisters. This is the place for the genuine article.

If I had seen Mrs. Moscheles at that ball I went to last night, where there were such quantities of tallow candles, and we had ham and potatoes for supper, and the boards were sprinkled after the first dance, not after the second (that would have been no use, the dust was so thick that you could hardly see the people), and they danced down the stove to the capital music of some worthy members of my band,—the whole thing got up by the Commercial Club, commonly called "The Parliament,"—and the ladies' dresses—no, but these baffle description—only, had I seen Mrs. Moscheles there, and she me, in my best English cravat too, I should just have collapsed for very shame; for on these occasions I positively cannot believe there is such a thing in the whole place as a gentleman. Now, what I should like of all things would be to go and enjoy myself at the fair; surely it could not be ungenteeler, but undoubtedly jollier; only, you see my rank as Musikdirector does not allow of my taking such liberties, a fact that the Burgomaster himself has strongly impressed upon me. And then we have the glorious rivalry between Düsseldorf and Elberfeld, which is twelve miles off; Düsseldorf styling itself Athens, and dubbing Elberfeld Rio de Janeiro or Augsburg. And then all the girls are plain; and that is quite a misfortune, or at least a grievance. So I really associate only with artists, and they are very good fellows. As for Immermann,[1] with whom I used to be on friendly terms, he is completely immersed in theatrical business,

[1] Immermann the poet and dramatist. Amongst his best-known works are "Münchhausen," and the epic poem of "Tristan and Isolde."

Uechtritz in æsthetics, and Grabbe in the bottle,— three things I don't much care for, least of all perhaps for æsthetics.

The other day I was asked to edit a musical review. I should have liked to call out the firm that made the request; for nothing seems to me more unsatisfactory or distasteful than a concern of that kind, in which you have to suit other people's pleasure and take all the annoyance to yourself. The other day I received from a local composer some songs with guitar accompaniment, for my opinion. The first began thus:—

whereupon the voice comes in, and towards the end of the letter the man asks me whether in my judgment Handel was really the great man he is usually taken to be. Now, would n't he do for the editor? What better qualification for the post than that song and that question?

But, to be serious again, my dear Moscheles, when you write tell me all you can about your new Overture to Joan of Arc, of which I have so far only been able to hear in a general way. Have you written anything besides the Overture, and if so, what? Are we not to have a third book of Studies? I do not believe there is in all Germany a single pianist, worthy or unworthy of the name, who does not know the first two books, and play them, — Heaven only knows how, to be sure, — and by publishing a third, you would really be conferring a boon on all musical people. Remember now, I want chapter and verse about everything you have been writing.

Among the new music you are constantly looking through, have you come across anything good? I have not seen anything that I quite liked. A book of Mazurkas by Chopin and a few new pieces of his are so mannered that they are hard to stand. Heller, too, has written two books of Songs that he had better have left unwritten. I so wish I could admire it all; but it is really so little to my taste, that I cannot. A few things there are, too, by some Berliners and Leipzigers, who would like to begin where Beethoven left off. They can "clear their throats" as he does, and "cough his cough," and that is just all. To me it is like riding across the fields after the rain; on horseback they can dash along splendidly, even if they do get splashed, but when they try to walk, they get stuck fast in the mud. I have heard "Gustave III." by Auber; in that kind of opera the music is fast becoming of secondary importance, — a good thing too. Yesterday I read in a French paper that Bellini is gazetted Knight of the Légion d'Honneur; Louise Vernet, whom I once upon a time admired so much, marries Delaroche the artist; and Urhan has written pianoforte pieces he calls "Lettres à Elle." But I dare say you know all that, as well as the good news that the "Œuvres complètes de Moscheles" are about to appear at Schlesinger's.

There, I am at the end of my paper just as I was going to begin in good earnest; it is quite as well, for I have nothing new to say, but only something old, — namely, my love to you all, and my longing to be with you once more. Well, next May I shall probably give one of my awkward knocks at your door. For the present, good-by; best love to Emily, Serena, and Felix, who I am sure speaks French by this time, or at any rate soon will. And now enough, — too much perhaps.

Ever yours,

FELIX M. B.

Moscheles sent Mendelssohn his Overture to Joan of Arc; and two Songs on words by Uhland, "The Smith" and "In Autumn."

DÜSSELDORF, March 25, 1835.

MY DEAR MOSCHELES, — A thousand thanks for your kindness in sending me the two Songs and the Overture, and for the nice letter which came with them. It is too good of you. In your busy life, with so many demands on your time, you actually copy out music for me, and take pleasure in giving me pleasure! The mere sight of the parcel gladdened my very heart; and now that I have the contents, I long to hear the whole Overture, instead of having to fancy the single parts linked together. Now I have a clearer conception of the whole work, and am particularly delighted with the French March in the middle, — which, I am sure, must have a capital effect, — then the theme in minor at the end, and indeed the whole idea and conception. The Allegro Spiritoso is, I suppose, the principal section of the work; at least I cannot fancy it otherwise. And what about the end? Do you finish in minor with the Funeral March, or are "all standards slowly lowered at the king's command"? The beginning of the minor March which you have written out for me is so fine that I long to know its conclusion. The March, I suppose, comes in towards the end; the trombones in answer to the muted Quartet must have a splendid effect.

You have given me nearly as much pleasure by the two Songs. They are so intrinsically German, not a bit French or English, never aiming at effect, and therefore producing the most agreeable effect upon me; for I cannot say how glad I am that you, in the midst of all your successes, have not lost the taste or love for such small, unobtrusive, beautiful songs. There is something truly artistic and truly German in that, — just what I delight to find in you. I like the Song in B major best, particularly the charming close, where the voice descends from F sharp while the accompaniment keeps on hammering away. So, too, the *piano* to the words "black forge" is delightful. In the Song in F, I particularly like the recurrence of the subject creeping in through the accompaniment at the words, "Ah, those were lovely dreams!" But will you allow me to mention a trifling matter with which I do not quite agree? There are a few *nuances* in the declamation, — or whatever else I may call it, — just at the beginning, to the words, "Yonder at the garden entrance," where the quiet fall of the melody appears out of keeping, and where, musically speaking, the two half-bars seem to drag somewhat. I fancy it would sound livelier if they were omitted, and the melody went on without delay, so that, in the following bars, the words would not be dwelt upon at such length. Thus the word "glad" would get into the first bar, and the word "chords" into the second. This is still more striking at the word "soul," in B major, where I feel confident the melody should go on without rest, as the verse goes on, — the word "again" belonging to "dost thou know," according to the meaning of the text. So, also, I was struck by the long pause preceding the words "look around," the accompaniment going on to A major, and then by the spinning out of the words "around them." I fancy you might leave out one or two bars altogether.

But when I remember that I am writing to you,

Moscheles, and that from me to you all this is very presumptuous, I am half afraid you will be offended — but no, I don't mean that either, for I know you would not take offence at my straightforwardness. If I tell you honestly where I think you have been less successful, it shows you that I am sincere where I appreciate, and that I thank you for all the rest.

What you say about Berlioz's Symphony is literally true, I am sure; only I must add that the whole thing seems to me so dreadfully slow, — and what could be worse? A piece of music may be a piece of uncouth, crazy, barefaced impudence, and still have some "go" about it and be amusing; but this is simply insipid and altogether without life.

Some studies of Hiller's I saw the other day I could not bring myself to like, either; which I am sorry for, because I am fond of him, and believe he has talent. But Paris, no doubt, is bad soil.

This page is to be devoted to my thanks for your kind letter, dear Mrs. Moscheles. You know how much I like London; so your pressing me to come is doubly kind. But I am sorry to say your letter arrived after I had decided to give up that pleasure this year. Klingemann will have told you so; and I need not add how sorry I am. Having, however, made up my mind to live and labor in Germany whilst I can, I could not refuse the conductorship of the Rhenish Musical Festival without materially injuring my position here; and as the Festival is held in June, — by which time I could not get back, — my favorite scheme has fallen to the ground. When I may take it up again I cannot say, but I trust it may be soon. Till then I must give up the extempore Fantasias for two performers, and the slow prestos, and the sugar-kaleidoscope, and the "Fall of Paris" knock. To lose all that for the sake of serious business is horrid; but how to help it?

There is an end of the paper, my dear Moscheles. Kindly accept the Overtures, and give me your opinion on them. The first has remained pretty nearly as it was; the two others are much altered. Let me hear all about your Concerto in C minor soon; I look forward to it with pleasure and impatience.

I must bid farewell, for to-day, to No. 3 Chester Place. Love to the children and the whole house.

F. MENDELSSOHN BARTHOLDY.

BERLIN, Aug. 13, 1835.

MY DEAR MOSCHELES, — I do not know how to thank you for your kind letter; it gave me the greatest pleasure, and I should certainly have answered it sooner; only, I really had neither mood nor leisure to write. You know my mother was taken very ill in Düsseldorf, and recovered but slowly, and she could only undertake the journey here with the greatest caution, I accompanying her. My anxiety, both before the journey and on the road, was so great that I could not collect my thoughts for anything, and I did not feel relieved till both parents once more settled down comfortably at home to their old habits. Now, thank God, all traces of past fatigues are fast disappearing, and they are so well, or rather so much better than before, that I breathe freely again. Anyhow, I should have written to you shortly, but to London; for I had no idea you were going to Hamburg so soon, and the news of your arrival quite took me by surprise; but now I should like to know all about your past and future movements. That you should think of going to St. Petersburg, I more or less expected, confident as I am that you would be worshipped there and overwhelmed with kindness. But how long do you mean to stay? When to start? To be sure, you return to England. And then I want to hear something of the past; for, capital as your lines about Aloys Schmidt and Benedict are, there must be something too to say about new publications by others; and above all I want full particulars of your own compositions, what pieces you are planning, and how your concert went off. Do write about it all when you have a leisure hour; you know what pleasure it gives me. Your last letter I showed my parents, and they fully appreciated your kind words. My father will add a few lines to these.

Your description of Aloys Schmidt's tallow-candle *soirée* and the conversation on sevenths was so graphic that I really could smell the tallow, hear the quartet, taste the green tea, feel the oppressive dulness, — in fact, it is as if all my senses had had their share in the proceedings. What you say of Liszt's harmonies is depressing. I had seen the thing at Düsseldorf, and put it aside with indifference because it simply seemed very stupid to me; but if that sort of stuff is noticed, and even admired, it is really provoking. But is that the case? I cannot believe that impartial people can take pleasure in discords or be in any way interested in them: whether a few reporters puff the piece or not, matters little; their articles will leave no more traces than the composition. What annoys me is that there is so little to throw into the other side of the balance; for what our Reissiger & Co. compose, though different, is just as shallow, and what Heller and Berlioz write is not music either, and even old Cherubini's "Ali Baba" is dreadfully poor and borders on Auber. That is very sad.

But what is the use of grumbling about bad music? As if it could ever take the lead, even if all the world were to sing it; as if there were no good music left! All such things, however, make me feel the obligation of working hard and of exerting myself to put into shape to the best of my abilities that which I fancy to be music. I do feel sometimes as if I should never succeed; and to-day I am quite dissatisfied with my work, and should just like to write my Oratorio over again from beginning to end. But I am quite decided to bring it out at Frankfurt next winter, and at the Düsseldorf Musical Festival at Whitsuntide; so I must finish it now. Besides, I think I have worked too long at it; at least, I am quite impatient to get to other things, so it is evidently high time to end. I have got to recopy the whole score, and make a good many alterations and additions, — rather a heavy piece of work that often tires me. In the course of the winter I am going to write a Symphony in A minor, and get my "Walpurgisnacht" ready for publication.

And what about the next book of "Studies"? I am quite longing for it, and so are all pianoforte-players. I wish you would let us have it soon. Don't you mean to do so? And how about the Sonata for four hands?

You know that I am going to spend next winter in Leipzig to conduct the Abonnement Concerts. I have only engaged myself from Michaelmas to Easter. I'm a little afraid of it, and can't fancy a residence there agreeable. My plans for next spring, after the Musical Festival, rather point towards the South than towards England. So I must trust to chance for bringing us together, and that is perhaps better than all planning for the future. Good-by.

Yours ever,

FELIX MENDELSSOHN BARTHOLDY.

My address for the present is Berlin; and from next September, Breitkopf & Härtel, Leipzig. Use it often.

At the close of the season Moscheles went to Hamburg with his family, from which place he announces to Mendelssohn his intention of visiting Leipzig for the purpose of seeing his mother, who was coming from Prague to meet him. He also speaks of his intention to give a concert in Leipzig.

LEIPZIG, Sept. 5, 1835.

MY DEAR MOSCHELES, — I hope and trust nothing may occur to prevent our once more spending a few happy days together. Your concert is being arranged, and so I shall have the twofold pleasure of seeing you and hearing your more important new works, and I need not tell you how much I shall enjoy that.

Your search after flowers in the arid regions of modern composition makes me quite melancholy. It is so disheartening to see how colorless the heroes of our day are. Sometimes it makes me feel inclined to think too indulgently of myself; at other times again the very reverse, and I feel thoroughly discouraged. Who is Mr. Elkamp who is writing a "Saint Paul"? Have you seen anything of his, and has it any merit or not?

If the Hamburgers look upon your appearance as an *intermezzo* between Chopin and Kalkbrenner, let them go to Jericho. I would soon put things into plain language, and ask them whether they consider the joint an *intermezzo* between mixed pickles, hashes, and fish patties, or whether it is not rather the other way. A comparison of that kind would, I believe, be most likely to come home to them. Kalkbrenner is the little fish patty.

Have you heard or seen anything of Lindenau the violinist? The last time I heard him, in Düsseldorf, I was exceedingly pleased with his playing. If you meet him, please remember me kindly to him, and ask whether he would come and play here. Good violinists seem to be scarce, and I should be glad if he would let us hear him soon. I am not quite clear as to the state of musical matters here. There seems to be plenty of music performed; but how much for the love of the thing, remains to be seen. That is, however, a vast subject, and we must discuss it accordingly, and rediscuss it, and say wise things about it; and may all that come to pass soon!

Just now Hauser comes in, and I tell him of my beautiful joke on Kalkbrenner; but he will have it that K. is more like an indigestible sausage, and I am to tell you so with his best love. Your kind offer of services reminds me of a favor you can do me on your way here. Klingemann wrote me the other day that he had had some money from you for me, and that you have a balance in my favor from Novello's payments for the "Melodies." If you could let my father have this on your way through Berlin, you would oblige me. Excuse my troubling you. I must end, or my letter won't be in time. Pardon these hurried, good-for-nothing lines. Be sure you bring all your newest compositions with you; mind you do, it will be such a treat for me. And now, best love to wife and children, and good-by. Forget not

Yours,

FELIX MENDELSSOHN BARTHOLDY.

On the 1st of October Moscheles arrived in Leipzig; there, as prearranged, he met his mother. The ten days passed in her company and in musical and friendly intercourse with Mendelssohn are amongst the happiest recorded in the diary. On the 2d of October he says: "I passed the evening with Felix; his friend Schleinitz, a lawyer, came in; he has a lovely tenor, and sang some of Felix's songs.[1] Then Felix and I played my 'Hommage à Handel' for two performers; all my Studies he knows by heart, and he plays them beautifully."

October 3. — "Rehearsal for the first Subscription Concert of the season. Mendelssohn appeared for the first time at the head of the Leipzig orchestra. He conducted with befitting dignity, exercising authority without pedantry, and was

[1] Schleinitz was a well-known figure in the musical world of Leipzig. He was an intimate friend of Mendelssohn's, and for many years indefatigable in his work as Director of the Leipzig Conservatorio.

most cordially seconded by the members of the orchestra."

In addition to Moscheles's diary we have his letters written from Leipzig to his wife, who, with her children, had remained in Hamburg on a visit to her relatives.[1] Moscheles writes of meeting "a retiring but interesting young man, Robert Schumann," and of "the admirable and unaffected playing of Clara Wieck," afterwards Madame Schumann. He shows us Mendelssohn's study, with "the bookcase,—a perfect storehouse of musical scores;" the writing-table, on which he notices the silver inkstand presented to Mendelssohn by the Philharmonic Society; the engravings on the wall; a delightful litter of scores and other music on the piano; "still," he says, "cleanliness and neatness prevailing everywhere." Then again we follow the two friends to the keyboard of the Erard, which stands in the middle of the room. They play, together and alternately, their latest compositions: some "Songs without Words," Moscheles's Concertos (Fantastique and Pathétique), and Mendelssohn's Overture, "Calm Sea and Prosperous Voyage." "Last night," says Moscheles, "we played my Overture and his Octet together; it went swimmingly, and when we parted he lent me his cloak, for fear I should catch cold after so many hot notes. This morning he was rewarded with an extra piece of that cake my mother brought from Prague for us."

[1] See "Life of Moscheles," vol. i. pp. 318 and following.

The above-mentioned cake, originally intended for the expectant family in Hamburg, was destined to be sacrificed to the appetites of a small party of belated travellers. Moscheles, Mendelssohn, and his sister Madame Dirichlet with her family, had travelled together from Leipzig to Berlin, and on arriving at half-past one o'clock in the morning they had found the Mendelssohn house in deep slumbers and the larder closed; it was there the cake met its pleasant fate. "Pleasanter still," says Moscheles, "was the awaking next morning. The meeting with the Mendelssohn family was quite touching; we embraced all round, and Felix's happiness and overflowing spirits were quite child-like. As for myself, I was received as affectionately as if I belonged to the family."

Though at first reluctant to delay his return to Hamburg, Moscheles finally yielded to the kindly pressure of his friends and remained with them.

Of his concert Moscheles wrote a glowing account; Mendelssohn indorses it in the following letter: —

LEIPZIG, Oct. 11, 1835.

I cannot forego the pleasure, dear Mrs. Moscheles, of sending you an account of the events of the last two days, although necessarily a short one, as I am beset by professional and non-professional visitors. It has really been too delightful, and such a pity you were not here to enjoy the treat

Moscheles gave us all. Those two days were indeed thoroughly musical ones, with everybody full of excitement and genuine enthusiasm.

Let me begin with the concert of the day before yesterday; you know the programme, and you also know how Moscheles plays. Well, then, directly after his "Concerto Fantastique" the shouts of applause began, and the noise lasted throughout the evening, and continued at yesterday's rehearsal, so that this evening's concert promises to be one of the most glorious, the Leipzig people being half crazed. Besides, you know, the room was the most crowded we have had for years; but what pleased me most was the intense interest and delight which pervaded the audience.

When we got to the end of our duet, — and it did go well, I assure you, — the most deafening acclamations broke forth, so that we played the last eight or ten bars without anybody, not even ourselves, being able to hear whether we did it correctly; nor did they leave off clapping and cheering till they had us out again, to perform a second duet — of graceful bows. And now you may fancy how madly they went on after Moscheles's "extempore playing." It is true he produced some things bordering on witchcraft, which to this day I have not been able to understand, although he pretends they were nothing; but it was quite delightful to see how excited and appreciative the audience were. An English lady, rather blue, wanted to be introduced, and gave vent to her enthusiasm, whilst a score of Leipzig ladies of all colors waited for her to make room. (And here is the proper place to inform you that Moscheles was struck on two separate occasions by the beauty of a Leipzig lady, and each time informed me of the fact, in a discreet whisper; whereupon I threatened to let you know, which I hereby do.) Well, then, the Leipzig ladies came to the balustrade of the orchestra, and Moscheles made them a bow; then came the dignitaries of this place; then one or other of the art critics, who gave detailed reasons for their praise; and lastly the committee of our concerts (consisting of twelve gentlemen — not one lady), to beg that they might hear the Overture to "Joan of Arc" once more at this evening's concert. A work of that kind has too many novel and striking points to be at once understood by band and audience, so that we look forward with delight to its repetition to-day. They have now played it four days in succession, and it will go to perfection; even at yesterday's rehearsal it seemed like a new piece, and fresh beauties were brought out. The duet, too, has to be repeated *by desire;* and as Moscheles had already promised to play his Concerto in G minor ("Blue Devils"),[1] we shall, I think, have a splendid night of it.

Let me just add that at yesterday's rehearsal

[1] The first movement of the G minor Concerto is styled "Malinconico."

Moscheles played his Concerto in a more masterly manner than I believe I have ever heard him play before, which is saying a great deal; the unanimous applause which followed must have given him some pleasure. It was the last piece of the rehearsal; the Overture had been played beautifully, and now we all — the unoccupied — formed a large circle around him. Mademoiselle Grabau, our *prima donna*, turned over the pages, the other singers standing close by; a Kammerherr,[1] who had expressly come from a distant place in the country, and who fancied himself a good pianist, kept his eyes fixed on Moscheles's fingers; the band exerted itself to the utmost, and Moscheles played quite wonderfully and delighted everybody. I only wish you and he could have seen the smiles and nods of the band and the audience, their secret looks of astonishment, and the unutterable surprise of the Kammerherr. Accustomed as Moscheles is to such demonstrations, he must have been struck by this outburst. As to myself, I cannot sufficiently tell you how I am enjoying his visit. Alas! it is coming to an end, as he is returning to you the day after to-morrow; but it was a happy time, long to be remembered, and always with delight.

I am again interrupted, and I expect Moscheles in an hour to take me to his mother's, where I am to play; so I am obliged to conclude, leaving him to give you verbally all the Leipzig news, which I

[1] Court Chamberlain.

should have preferred to do myself in this letter, if the Hamburg mail did n't leave at ten o'clock.

Ever yours,

FELIX MENDELSSOHN BARTHOLDY.

Mendelssohn again writes to Mrs. Moscheles:—

If you want to be angry with Moscheles for giving us another day, you must be angry with all the inmates of the Leipzigerstrasse No. 3; for they are all at fault. He wanted to proceed at once, although he only arrived last night, or rather this morning at half-past one o'clock; but we all bent the knee of persuasion, in addition to which the police would not deliver his passport. Then, again, you will have him in Hamburg, Holland, and London, whereas we shall have to part to-morrow, probably for a long time. In a word, I for one begged and prayed to my heart's content; put yourself in my place, you would have done the same. Moscheles, on his return, will give you all our cordial messages; it is post-time. I close, and trust you will not frown on

Yours sincerely,

FELIX MENDELSSOHN BARTHOLDY.

Moscheles remained three days with the Mendelssohns. To none did he give greater pleasure than to the elder Mendelssohn, who, afflicted as he was with partial blindness, derived the keenest enjoyment from music. On the last evening of

Q. D. B. V.
SVMMIS AVSPICIIS
POTENTISSIMI SAXONIAE REGIS
AC DOMINI
ANTONII
DOMINI NOSTRI CLEMENTISSIMI
ET
PRINCIPIS SERENISSIMI
FRIDERICI AVGVSTI
DVCIS SAXONIAE SOCII IMPERII CELSISSIMI
IN VNIVERSITATE LITERARVM LIPSIENSI
RECTORE ACADEMIAE MAGNIFICO
D. CAROLO FRIDERICO GVENTHERO
FACVLT. IVRID. ORDINARIO. PROF. IVR. PRIMARIO. ECCLES. CATHEDR. MERSEB. CAPITVLARI. SVPREMAE
CVRIAE SAXON. CONSILIARIO. ORDIN. SAXON. VIRTVT. CIVIC. EQVITE CAET.
PROCANCELLARIO
MAVRITIO GVILIELMO DROBISCHIO
MATHEM. PROF. P. O. SOCIETT. IABLONOV. OECON. NATVR. SCRVTATT. LIPS. ET PHYSICO-MEDICAE DRESD. SODALI
DECANO
CHRISTIANO AVGVSTO HENRICO CLODIO
PHILOSOPHIAE PRACT. PROF. PVBL. ORD. COLLEGII PRINC. MAI. SENIORE
VIR CLARISSIMVS
FELIX MENDELSSOHN-BARTHOLDY
CONCENTVS MVSICI APVD LIPSIENSES DIRECTOR
OB INSIGNIA IN ARTEM MVSICAM MERITA
HONORIS CAVSA
PHILOSOPHIAE DOCTOR ET BONARVM ARTIVM MAGISTER
CREATVS
ET HAC TABVLA PVBLICA DECLARATVS EST.

P. P. DOMIN. IVDICA A. R. S. MDCCCXXXVI.

LIPSIAE
TYPIS STARITZII TYPOGR. ACAD.

17. Fac-simile of Diploma given to Mendelssohn by the University of Leipzig, March 20, 1836.

Moscheles's stay, he and Mendelssohn were improvising together; as the hour of departure approaches, the latter suddenly breaks in with the familiar bugle-call of the post-chaise. Moscheles answers with a solemn valedictory Andante; again he is interrupted by the warning notes of the bugle, and pressing forward, the two performers end with a *brillant* Finale. These days were amongst the last that Mendelssohn's father was destined to enjoy. A heavy blow was in store for the Mendelssohn family and the wide circle of their friends. Abraham Mendelssohn died quite suddenly on the 19th of November.

Berlin, Nov. 25, 1835.

My dear Friend, — We have lost my father. He breathed his last tranquilly and peacefully on the 19th, in the morning, at half-past ten o'clock. He had long since wished it might be so, and God has heard him. May He give us strength to live on without him, and bear up under a loss we can scarcely realize! My mother and sisters are well; my mother an example to all, looking at the future with courage and fortitude. It was owing to you that I saw my father the last time, and for that I thank you. The remembrance of those two happy days is like a blessing that I shall carry through life. You knew him, and can judge how, with him, light and happiness have gone from me. I will strive to live as he would have wished me to live, had he been amongst us. To your wife my father was always sincerely attached, and grateful for all her kindness to him and to us all. She, too, has lost a friend, and so have all those who knew him well.

I must return to Leipzig in a few days, and do my best to get through my duties there.

Good-by. Yours,

F. Mendelssohn Bartholdy.

On his return to Leipzig he resumed his work with untiring energy; on the 22d of May of the following year (1836) he conducted the first performance of his Oratorio, "Saint Paul," at the Düsseldorf Festival; he next went to Frankfurt to take the direction of the Saint Cecilia Choir, in place of his friend Schelble, who was incapacitated through illness. Here he first met that other Cecilia who was henceforth to become his guiding star, and who was eventually to exchange her name for his. They were engaged on the 9th of September, Mendelssohn's mother communicating the welcome news to the Moscheles family.

Frankfurt, July 20, 1836.

My dear Friend, — It is an age since I wrote to you last; but it was a monotonous age, and I was not in a mood to write about it or anything else. Besides, you know that however much time passes without your hearing from me, there is not a day that does not in some way or other bring me nearer to you or remind me of your friendship, your work, and your life so beneficial to us all. I have not yet thanked you for that good kind letter of yours which reached me through Klingemann at the Music Festival, with your congratulations on its success. How the Oratorio went off you have heard long ago. There was much that pleased me at the performance, and much that dissatisfied me; and even now I am at work on certain parts of the pianoforte arrangement, which is to appear shortly, and on the orchestral score, so much is there that completely fails to express my idea,—in fact, does not even come near it. You have often advised me not to alter so much, and I am quite aware of the disadvantages of so doing; but if, on the one hand, I have been fortunate enough to render my idea in some parts of my work, and have no desire to change those, I cannot help striving, on the other hand, to render my idea in other parts, and, if possible, throughout.

But the task begins to weigh heavily upon me, as I am gradually more and more attracted by other work, and I wish I could look back upon the Oratorio as finally completed. Well, I hope in two months, at the outside, to send you the P. F. arrangement. But where will you be then? What a thing it is to be separated by land and sea! I hear a great deal about you and your work through people coming from London, and I read about it in the musical papers; besides, you write occasionally, and so does Klingemann; but if I compare all that with our meeting in Leipzig, or with those days in England, when it was a matter of course that I should know how you spent every morning and afternoon, then letter-writing does appear a very poor substitute. I suppose you will be going to the seaside on the English coast. I, too, am ordered sea-bathing, and shall have to swallow the bitter pill of a regular cure, and go in about a fortnight to Scheveningen, or rather to the Hague, where I can live quietly away from the bathing community, and drive out every morning to the sea for my ablutions. In the first days of September, when the Subscription Concerts begin, I must be back in Leipzig.

I wish I could finish a few Symphonies and that sort of thing in the course of the year, and more still I long to write an Opera; but of that I am afraid there is not the least prospect. I am looking in vain throughout all Germany and elsewhere for some one to help me realize this and other musical plans, and I despair of finding him. It is really absurd to think that in all Germany one should not be able to meet with a man who knows the stage and writes tolerable verses; and yet I positively believe there is none to be found. Altogether, this is a queer country. Much as I love it, I hate it in certain respects. Look at the musical men of this place, for instance; their doings are quite shameful. Considering the size and importance of the town, there is really a fair muster of excellent musicians, men of reputation and talent, who might do good work, and who, one would think, would do it willingly; so far that is the good side of Germany, but the fact is, they do nothing, and it were better they did not live together, and grumble, and complain, or brood over their grievances till it 's enough to give one the blues. Ries is by this time in England, I suppose; he considers he does not meet with due appreciation, and finds fault with the musicians, and yet does nothing to improve them. Aloys Schmidt takes his ease in the country, sighs over mankind in general,— a poor race at the best, full of envy and malice, —forgetting all the while that he, too, belongs to it. Hiller is here just now. People discuss wildly whether he is a great pianoforte-player or not, but they don't go to hear him, and fancy that makes their judgment all the more impartial; so he, too, is leaving for Italy. The only man who succeeds is Guhr, who knows least and is n't good for much; but he has a will of his own, and enforces it *bon gré, mal gré,* and the whole town lives in fear of him. But all that is bad, and the German Diet should interfere; for where so many musicians congregate in one place, they ought to be forced by the authorities to give us the benefit of a little music, and not only their philosophical views about it.

What have you been composing, and what are your plans for the autumn? I am anxious, too, to know how you have treated your scoring of the Bach Concerto. Taubert has, I suppose, been drowned in the whirl of pianists, and was little noticed. It could scarcely have been otherwise; I always thought he had not much talent. Thalberg, whom you portray so admirably, I should like to hear again; he must have developed wonderfully.

And do you know that my Oratorio is to be published in London, at Novello's, and that his letter about it dropped from the skies into my hands the other day? And do you know, also, that Rossini, with Pixis, Francilla, the Swedish composer Lindblad, and the Polish straw-fiddler Gusikow, have all been through Frankfurt? But I must leave off writing and chatting. Good-by; best love to wife and children, and don't forget

Yours,

F. Mendelssohn Bartholdy.

On the 14th of August Moscheles writes: —

My dear Felix, — You ask me about my scoring of the Bach Concerto. Well, it seemed to me that one might give it a kind of new varnish, by doing for it what Mozart had done with such perfect taste for the "Messiah," when he added wind-instruments to the score. Only, fully aware as I was of the poverty of my pen as compared with that of the master, I naturally hesitated. If now, however, I have followed the great example before me, the worst that can be said of me is that I am but a poor imitator; and consoling myself with that reflection, I wrote Parts for one Flute, two Clarinets, two Bassoons, and two Corni. I mainly intended this wind-accompaniment to take the same position in the Concerto which is taken by the organ in the performance of a Mass.

Hauser kept his promise very punctually, and sent me two more of Bach's Concertos, — one for three, and one for two pianofortes. I will shortly let you know what I already possess of Bach's concert-music; perhaps you can help me to complete my collection. My thirst for more of his work is simply unquenchable.

Of the pianoforte-players, Thalberg is really the most interesting. Sound and genuine in his style of playing, he does not seem to seek after effect, however much he may do so in reality. In his combinations, capricious and fantasia-like as they are, all follows and develops itself so naturally that one easily overlooks the lack of unity and a certain Italian mannerism. In 1826 I gave him some instruction; and at that time already I became aware that he would little need me to do great things, — *sans comparaison*, like a certain Berlin youth, who soon threw aside all leading-strings, and donned the purple.

I find that at my age my fingers require to practise most carefully the exercises of former years, in order to keep pace with the times. I can manage to preserve them pliable and elastic, but

I cannot make them any longer than they are; and that is just the road that modern pianists, like Chopin, Thalberg, etc., have taken, in order to develop their technique. To play your music, I have also to stretch my fingers to the fullest extent; but there they obey more naturally, because the mechanical construction of your passages is of secondary importance, as compared to the spirit which dictates them.

Moscheles, in thanking Mendelssohn for his last letter, says: —

"It is with so much pleasure I see your handwriting, your ideas and views have so much charm for me (although I occasionally think they may yet ripen to full maturity), I so fully recognize your genius, and am personally so much attached to you, that the word 'friendship' but inadequately expresses my feelings. Similarly, it is a source of happiness to me to know that your thoughts are often with me, aware, as I am, how constantly you are surrounded by an admiring circle of friends."

In reference to the preparations for a performance of "Saint Paul" in England, he says: —

"I am glad to find that all promises well for your Oratorio in England. Novello, Sir George Smart, and the whole profession are looking forward to its production with sympathy and interest. Like Hercules, you have throttled Envy while still in the cradle.

"Klingemann, Smart, and Novello are busy directing Mr. Ball, the translator. I have offered to correct the proofs, but have not yet received them."

SPEIER, April 6, 1837.

MY DEAR FRIEND, — Forgive my not having written for so long; the fact that it is a week since I was married, and that this is my first letter to a friend, must be my excuse. I need not tell you, and could not, if I tried, how the events of last year have added new prospects of happiness to my life, how all that is good has become doubly dear to me, all that is bad easier to put up with, how happy were the last months, how heavenly the last days! Looking back to the past and planning for the future, my thoughts have often reverted to you in friendship and affection, and to the happy hours spent with you. Believe me, I am truly grateful to you and your wife, and can never forget how many kindnesses you have at all times heaped on me. I have heard about you, both from Schumann and Bennett, but more particularly from Klingemann, who in his last letter describes some of your *soirées*, and your playing of Scarlatti, Handel, and Bach. It must have been delightful · and what is more delightful still, he drops a word about new "Studies" that you are going to play on one of these evenings. So you have at last written some; you cannot fancy how impatient I am to get them, what a treat it will be to me, and how refreshing to have something new to study. For really the piano music of the present day is such that I cannot make up my mind to play it through more than once; it is so desperately empty and poor that I usually get tired of it on the first page. I positively dislike Thalberg's work as regards the composition; and the good piano passages seem to me of no earthly use, so little soul is there in them. I could no more play his music than I could ever make up my mind to play a note of Kalkbrenner's; it goes against my nature, and I should feel mean if I attempted such fingerwork with a serious face. Chopin's new things, too, I don't quite like, and that is provoking. So, you see, it is doubly pleasant to think of the old "Studies" and to look forward to new ones. When shall we have them, and will there be more than one book?

Your wife, I suppose, I had better not address, for I am sure she is dreadfully angry; and, to say the truth, I am rather afraid of her. Nevertheless I do address her, for I want to speak of *my* wife, and say I hope she will not visit my sins upon her; on the contrary, she must be ready to like her and to love her a little when she becomes acquainted with her; and truly my dear Cécile deserves it, and I think I need not make any appeal to your wife, but simply introduce her and say, "This is Cécile,"—the rest will follow naturally. And do you know, it is quite possible I may bring her to you soon. I have had an invitation from Birmingham to conduct my "Saint Paul" at the Festival, and feel much inclined to accept. If I come, it may be in the autumn, or perhaps sooner, about the middle of August. But shall you be in England then? That is usually the time when you are away; it would be too great a pity if we were n't to meet. I cannot ask you to let me know about your plans,—for such a correspondent as I am can beg for pardon, but not for an answer; so send me word through Klingemann. But if you have leisure, and are disposed to treat me to a few lines, please address, all through the summer, care of M. T. Herz, Frankfurt.

If we meet this year, as I do hope we shall, I shall have several new things to show you. I have worked a good deal lately, and mean to be still more industrious. I shall send your wife a new book of Songs which is to appear in a few days, as soon as I get it.

And now good-by, my dear, dear friend; best love to your wife, and to the children if they have n't forgotten me and the carnations. If you see Klingemann tell him that I will shortly write to him, perhaps from Strassburg, where I am going to-morrow, from there to Freiburg and Bâle, and so back to Frankfurt. And now that I must end,

I feel as if everything yet remained to be said. Forget not

Yours,

F. MENDELSSOHN BARTHOLDY.

In September of this year Mendelssohn went to Birmingham, where he conducted the Festival. To their mutual regret Mendelssohn and Moscheles did not meet in England on that occasion, as the latter had left London for Germany at the close of the season.

LEIPZIG, Dec. 12, 1837.

MY DEAR MOSCHELES, — I cannot say I feel much of a correspondent to-day, so engrossed am I with the new life around and within me. This year, with all it has brought me, has been the happiest of my existence, and I daily appreciate the blessings it has bestowed. For the last week I have been installed with my Cécile in our own new quarters, everything has been made neat and comfortable, we have already had eight Subscription Concerts, and a performance of the Messiah in the Church, and I have a variety of work in my head and some on paper. So, you see, my occupations are much the same as usual, and the pressure from without at times greater. And yet nothing now upsets or troubles me, because my home is so happy and peaceful. So I trust you will forgive my long silence, if you ever resented it.

Of late I have spent some of my happiest hours with your new "Studies," the first proofs of which Kistner sent me. I had already got the engraver to send me whatever he could just spare, a sheet at a time; that gave me but a very superficial acquaintance with them, but I was too impatient to wait. Now I have had to return my copy, after correcting a number of mistakes, to Kistner, who is over-anxious about the work, and still delays its ultimate appearance. However, I have had the whole thing in my hands for a day, and have enjoyed it thoroughly; as soon as I have a copy to myself, I intend practising my piano properly, and mastering the Studies, for it is a long time since I had any piano music I wanted to play over and over again; so you can fancy how I enjoy something new, to which I can give my whole heart.

I cannot go into details, not having a copy before me; but this much I know, that my greatest favorites begin at "Contradiction." The whole piece in D flat major is so bright, and towards the end positively makes me laugh when it goes into D major and the whole story is repeated first in D major and then in D flat minor. And then the last bar *fff* is glorious. Quite your own self is that tender one in G major, just as if I heard you talk and play. But my greatest favorite is the "Nursery Tale," so graceful and sprightly; above all, I like the part where the deep bass notes double the melody, as if a big bassoon or some other growler of an instrument came in; and then the first transition to B major and the return to E flat and the very last bars *leggiero*, — all that has fixed itself once for all in my mind. How very much I like the "Bacchanali," "Terpsichore," and in fact all of them, you can imagine. I am particularly struck by the difference between these and your former Studies; — not that I love the old ones less, but the new ones are for quite a different class of players, far in advance of the former; here the technical difficulties have become of secondary importance, and the intrinsic merits of the work have to be brought out. Once more a thousand thanks, and may you give us many more of the same kind!

Did you hear anything good in the musical line during your stay in Hamburg last summer? Our concerts led to my becoming acquainted with some of the musical men there, but they were not much to speak of. In fact, there is a lack of good new musical productions everywhere, and that tells on our concerts here.

This winter Clara Novello is giving us a fresh start, the public cordially greeting her as a new and most welcome acquisition. She makes *la pluie et le beau temps*. But where are we to get a new Symphony from? May I address your wife quite at the bottom of this page, and write down a Song for her?

Dec. 12, 1837.

Dear Mrs. Moscheles, — Though I don't know whether you still care for me or my Songs, yet,

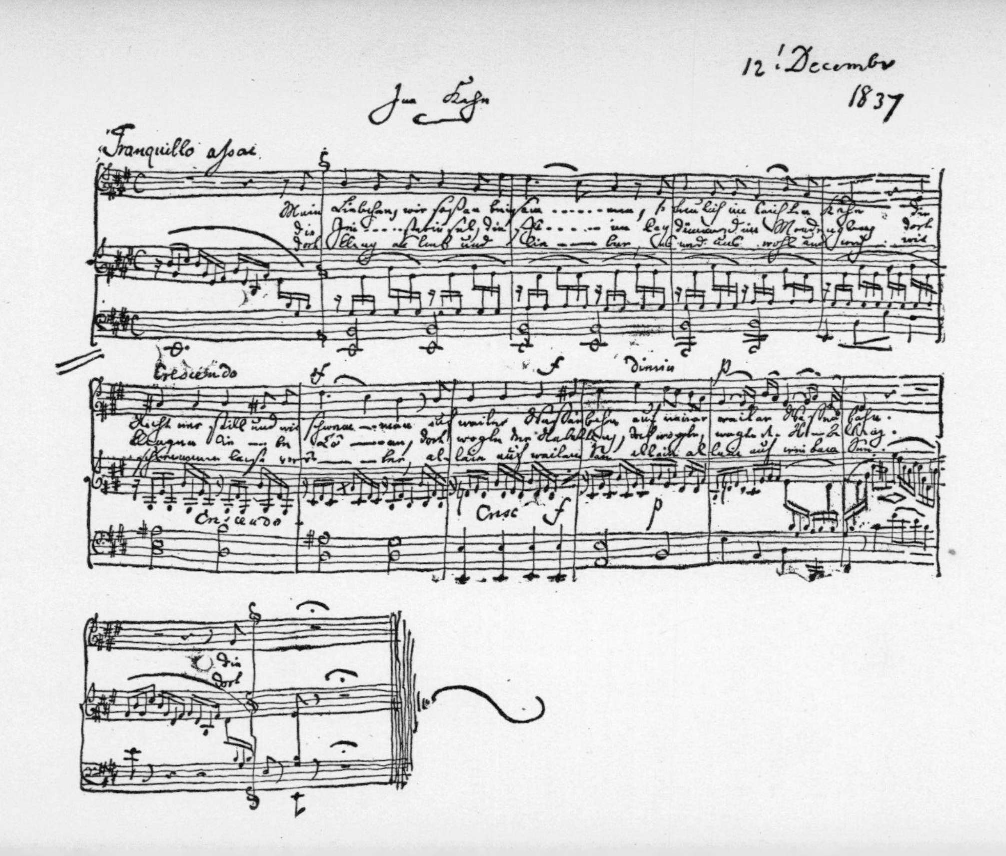
12! December
1837
Tranquillo assai
Crescendo
Dimin
Cresc

from old habit, I have written this one down for you, whether you sing it or not; but I do wish you would. What a pity we missed each other this time in England! I could not get it into my head that we were really not to meet; and yet, with every day of my stay in London, the fact was painfully evident. My wife wishes to write herself to thank you for your kind words. It was dreadful to have to leave her in Germany. It would have been my greatest joy to show her England properly; but so much is certain, I have made up my mind not to leave her again at Düsseldorf when I have to go to Rotterdam. It was too abominable.

I have only this corner left to bid you good-by, and to beg for a sign of life and friendship when your time permits.[1] May we soon have a happy meeting! Yours,

FELIX MENDELSSOHN BARTHOLDY.

On the 23d of December Moscheles writes: —

Your letter of the 12th broke in on me like a ray of sunshine piercing an autumn fog. Were I subject to the blues, like so many sufferers in this fog-ridden city, your cheerful lines would have set me up for any length of time.

Your appreciation of my "Studies" gives me much pleasure. I did not feel called upon to aim at popularity with the general public, nor did I

[1] See Illustration, No. 23.

venture to believe that my work addressed itself to the more restricted circle of connoisseurs. That you, of all the Select, should welcome me with a Bravo, strengthens my faith in myself. Delighted I am, too, to find that you, with your master eye, should at once have hit on the passages that seem to me my more successful inspirations.

We cannot get over our regrets to have missed you in London and Birmingham; your triumphs in the latter place are being echoed all over England. Your "Saint Paul," your pianoforte Concerto, and your performances on the organ, one and all, are unreservedly praised. I am glad to see that your Oratorio is announced by the Sacred Harmonic Society as "the popular Oratorio." We so-called Directors of the Philharmonic Society are thirsting for something new in the line of Symphonies or Overtures. It is as hopeless a task to satisfy the wishes of the Society as it was in times gone by for the Danaïdes to fill their tub. Some would have us supply them with half a dozen posthumous Symphonies of Beethoven, complete or fragmentary; others want a place found on the programme for every attempt at composition made by native talent.

You have promised us your A major Symphony in its new shape, and we mean to keep you to your word, and hope you will not let us wait long. It is a great favorite of mine, and I feel as if I were going to meet a beautiful girl in a new dress, and were wondering whether that would make me admire her more than before. *Nous verrons, nous entendrons.* In the mean while I hold in safe keeping my Beauty attired as I first knew her (the original score), and remain faithful to her.

Liszt writes from Milan that several of his compositions are to be published in London, and that he intends dedicating one of them to me. May my fingers grow by then! He wishes to become better known in this country, as he proposes coming here shortly.

The "Gazette Musicale" exalts Berlioz's Requiem above all music of all times. A new vista, it says, is opened! You know I am not a believer in this genius; tell me whether anything of his has been to your taste. Good-by; if my letter is welcome, reward me by soon letting me have one in return.

Ever your friend,

I. MOSCHELES.

BERLIN, June 26, 1838.

MY DEAR FRIEND,—I want your advice. You know that five years ago Erard presented me with one of his grand pianos. I took it first to Berlin, then to Düsseldorf, and lastly to Leipzig. Owing to such frequent shiftings, and possibly to some bad treatment, it is not fit for use in public, and not even to be depended on at home. In answer to my inquiry Erard suggests that I should send it to England to be repaired. I have ascertained that the Saxon Custom-house would allow it to be returned free of duty. Erard, on his side, has obtained the same leave in England; but the carriage there and back would come to a hundred and thirty odd thalers, and as that is about half what a new piano would cost me here, the question arises, Can I really expect a substantial improvement from the repairs? Give me your candid opinion on this.

You know I shall have to play in public occasionally in the course of the winter; and for that purpose, as well as for music at home, I want an instrument with a perfectly even and precise touch, responding freely and fully to my wants and wishes. The tone has retained its original power and beauty, and I should indeed be happy if the defective parts of the mechanism could be repaired. That, you see, is just the question; and as I am sure that similar cases must have come under your notice, I write to you for advice. If it could be done, I should think no sacrifice too great to preserve an instrument with such a splendid tone. As it is, however, I cannot use it at all; and last winter I had to play on borrowed pianos, — and very poor ones too. I ought to apologize for troubling you; but you alone know exactly what I desire and expect to find in a piano, and so to your judgment I appeal.

I suppose you know, through Hensel, that we are staying at my mother's, and are spending delightful days with her and my sisters. I cannot say that my visit to Cologne was quite pleasant this time. You see I have lost the taste for anything I cannot share with my wife. I get to feel so restless and impatient that I am always calculating the day and hour of my return, and can think of nothing else.

We shall go back to Leipzig in August. And you, — where are you going this summer? When shall we see you in Germany? All those who like good music are longing for you. And what are you composing? I am working on a Symphony in B flat.[1] I have gone forward a step since last year, and could I but have the benefit of your opinion on my work occasionally, I should get along more rapidly. I have composed a few new Quartets for string instruments, a Sonata with violin and one with violoncello, besides a few trifles not published in England that I am waiting for an opportunity to send you.

Good-by, and best love to you all. I do hope the day may not be too far distant when I can introduce my Cécile to your wife. Pray tell her so. Fanny and I are making much music together; the day after to-morrow we are going to do my new Psalm in E flat. Her playing is more masterly than ever. Good-by once more, my dear friend, and may we soon meet again.

Yours,

FELIX MENDELSSOHN BARTHOLDY.

[1] This Symphony, so often referred to in Mendelssohn's letters of this time, has either entirely disappeared or was converted into the initial movement of the "Lobgesang."

Moscheles and his wife communicated on the subject of the piano with Mr. Erard, who at once expressed his readiness to present Mendelssohn with a new instrument. Writing to Mendelssohn on the subject, Moscheles says: —

"I shall choose an instrument for you myself, not omitting to bear in mind your favorite *arpeggio* passages, through which the melody seems to push its way. In other words, I shall test the piano with this passage from your Concerto, —

BERLIN, July 11, 1838.

MY DEAR FRIEND, — I enclose the certificate for Mr. Hogarth, addressed to you as you desire; also a few lines to him, which please forward with the enclosure when you have obliged me by reading and revising it and putting it into good English. I am afraid my English is very rusty; and as with you, such certificates are very frequently printed and published, I would rather no blunders were allowed to go forth to the world. So please turn them out one and all. I not only request you, but I hereby authorize you, to correct and to alter any and every thing, and to endow me with the right ideas expressed in an elegant style.

"From," "by," "while," have become so many unknown quantities to me; and I feel as nervous when I meet with them as I always do in the presence of distinguished strangers. Nor do I know whether I have said too little or too much. In the first case, put a few sforzandos; if it is the other way, soften a little. In fact, lend me a helping hand, as you have so often done before. Let us hope that, after all that, Mr. Hogarth's purpose may be served. How much I am indebted to you for the great service you have done me about the piano! But can I really accept it without further ceremony? I can't help feeling a doubt, though on the other hand I have the greatest desire to do so, as I am sadly in want of a good instrument. Would it not be meeting the difficulty half-way if I sent my piano to be repaired? For, after all, it might be possible to put it into good condition; and that would be to our mutual advantage. If the result was unsatisfactory I might still accept the kind offer of a new one. How would that do, my dear Moscheles? To be sure, I should rely on your judgment as to the completeness of the result. Or do you think I should simply accept the new one, taking Erard at his word, — such as I have it from Mrs. Moscheles, — and refer to her letter, in writing to him about it? Somehow or other I don't seem to find the right way of putting it to him; so I am just waiting till I hear from you. You know you are my helper and adviser; may you never get tired of the office!

So you are going to remain in England all through the summer. What a pity that it was last year, not this, that I had to be there! When I do not find you at home, it seems just as if I had not been to London at all.

I am surprised to hear of Döhler's being lionized. His playing only interested me the first time; afterwards he seemed to me very cold and calculating, and rather dull. What very different stuff Liszt and Chopin are made of! Why has Chopin never been to England? He has more soul in his little finger than all Döhler has from top to toe,—at least so it seemed to me. And Spontini!—do tell me all about him. I should so like to see what figure he cuts in London. Does he listen to music properly? Does he sometimes play himself, or does he there too give himself the airs of a big idol who may now and then devour a musician, but otherwise never moves a muscle? And does he deck himself out with all his decorations? How was Bennett's new Concerto, of which he writes to me, received at the Philharmonic? And how did Mrs. Shaw sing? You know she is coming to Leipzig this year; just give me a line or two about her. Miss Novello has had a marvellous success here. And now good-by.

Yours ever,

FELIX MENDELSSOHN BARTHOLDY.

Moscheles writes: —

"Bennett's F minor Concerto is an excellent piece of work, and was received very warmly at the Philharmonic; that he has taken you for his model is, however, evident throughout. I have also made acquaintance with Henselt's Studies, and find them very interesting and useful, although in style and form not varied enough. Anyhow, I prefer even the romantic sighs of love-warbling composers to the aggressive audacity of those torturers of harmony who would take the universe by storm. Chopin's Studies have much charm for me, although there is a good deal in them that appears unscholarlike to me. I like the new set better than the former ones; so far I have never had an opportunity of hearing him play."

LEIPZIG, Oct. 28, 1838.

MY DEAR FRIEND, — Bennett brought me your very kind letter last week. A thousand thanks for it; a thousand thanks, too, for always being so true a friend, and occasionally telling me so. A letter from you fortifies me for weeks; and what you write about yourself and others is so much to the point, so absolutely yourself, that I can almost hear you talking, and myself saying how right you are, and how much I like listening to you. Were I but a little milder, and a little more impartial, and a little cleverer, and a little more of a good many other things, I might also have as clear a judgment as you; but I am so easily put out, and I get so impatient, where you appreciate what is good for its own sake, and look on what is bad as capable of improvement.

I am so glad to hear you are at work, and of all things composing a Concerto. What key is it in? What form? How difficult? When shall we get it? Tell me all about it. Have you composed anything lately; and if so, what? As for me, those troublesome measles have quite thrown me back, as you thought they would. Even now, my eyes are not quite the thing, and I am still so sensitive that the least exertion knocks me up. With all that, my room-door is always on the move, like a toll-bar or a baker's door; and three weeks' enforced captivity and idleness have put everything into such confusion that I do not see my way out of all the work that has accumulated. I had intended publishing several things at this time, instead of which here I am correcting parts, marking tempos, and attending to the long list of *odiosa* that are always sure to take a dire revenge on the man who dares neglect them. I have written three new violin Quartets that I wish I could show you, because I am pleased with them myself, and should so like to have your opinion. A new Symphony, too, I hope to finish soon. My Serenade, and the other pianoforte piece in B minor,[1] you will perhaps come across; if so, you

[1] Rondo in B minor.

must be indulgent, and look at them through those friendly spectacles of yours.

And now I have an urgent request in reference to my piano. You ask how I am satisfied with it; and beyond that question I have heard nothing whatever of it since it left Hamburg. I wrote to Erard, thanking him for his kind intention, as communicated by you, and saying how pleased I was at the prospect of having a new piano. The old one left Hamburg on the 10th of August, but I have not yet had a line from Erard, no notice of its arrival, — in fact, nothing. I should be much obliged if you would let me know by return of post how matters stand, — whether I shall get the old one back or a new one, when it is to leave London, and so on. Meanwhile I have to make shift with a miserable old thing that goes out on hire, and tough work it is.

We have quite an English congress here just now. Mrs. Shaw has made many friends by her beautiful singing, and the public is looking forward with great interest to Bennett's new things. Clara Novello has been here too, and gave a concert which was well attended. On this occasion all manner of artistic rivalries and petty bickerings came to light, that would much better have remained in the dark. No, really, when these dear musicians begin to abuse one another, and to indulge in invective and backbiting, I could forswear all music, or rather all musicians. It does make me feel just like a cobbler; and yet it seems to be the fashion. I used to think it was only the way with the hacks of the profession; but the others are no better, and it takes a decent fellow with decent principles to resist the pernicious influence. Well, on the other hand, all this serves to show up what is good; and, by way of contrast, one doubly appreciates good art, good artists, letters from you, and—after all, this world of ours is not so bad.

Farewell, my dear friend; love from me and my wife to yours. How I wish we could soon be all together! Love to the children too.

Ever yours,

FELIX MENDELSSOHN BARTHOLDY.

Moscheles, in speaking of a "Concerto Pastorale" which he is composing, says:—

"You can fancy how careful I had to be lest I should run my humble craft on to that mighty rock, the 'Sinfonia Pastorale,' and be dashed to pieces. But you know there are buildings of various dimensions; and if you cannot erect churches, you must be content to build chapels. So I made the venture.

"In my Concerto, the movements are as follows: the Andantino con moto, 3-8 time, is descriptive of holiday-making and rural festivity. The whole village is rejoicing; all, from the farmer to the laborer, have donned their Sunday attire. Next comes an Allegretto in F major, 2-4 time. The rustic piper fills the air with joyous strains; the village beauty and her swain are rapt in dreams of coming bliss. After that, the Adagio. The church bells are calling the congregation to their devotions, and the bride and bridegroom to the fulfilment of their wishes. The ceremony is over, their destinies are linked, and they are greeted by the distant echoes of the Allegretto. It grows livelier as it bursts forth in D major, inviting to harmless merrymaking. Finally, a whirlwind of octaves sets lads and lasses skipping and dancing in boisterous glee. The newly married couple go through a dance of honor with due decorum, and the rural *fête* is brought to a happy close."

DEC. 10, 1838.

A thousand thanks, my dear friend, for your kind letter and all the trouble you have taken about the piano, — in fact, for all the love and kindness you always show me. To you alone I am indebted for that instrument, or rather you and your wife, who put the matter before Erard with so much tact and diplomacy; and it is only now, since I enjoy the happiness of playing on an instrument so full and rich in tone, that I realize how hard I should have found it to accustom myself to any other. So you see, my dear friend, how much I am in your debt. It is just as usual. "Thank you," is all I can say; but you know how much more I feel.

But now to the most important part of your letter, — that which refers to Weimar. Upon my word, it is not an easy matter to give you a proper answer to your questions. When I think of your life in London, your independent position at the head of the musical profession, and your never-ceasing activity in public, and then again of Weimar, with its petty Court, and its still pettier "Hofmarschall" and "Intendanz" that superintend nothing, — when I think of the littleness that pervades everything, it would be madness to advise you to go. When I remember, on the other hand, your telling me that you had never wished to remain all your life in England, but rather to return to your own country and devote yourself to your art and your friends (and I believe that in your place I should feel as you do); and when I take into account that in Germany one town is about as good as another, — all small but sociable, — that the appointment is one of the best of its kind, that to you it would be an acquisition to have an orchestra at your disposal, to us to have a man like you in Hummel's place, and secure a musician of your standing for Germany, — then I cannot help being in favor of Weimar. As far as I know, social resources are very limited there. The Court circle is the best, not to say the only one; there you still meet with intelligence and culture, — a relic of former days, — but that, too, is on the decline, and whether your wife would like it seems to me very doubtful. On the other hand, the orchestra is said to be excellent, and the singers at the Opera good; the Grand

Duchess is a stanch friend to anybody she once likes, and with that, fairly musical herself; not very much to do, but enough opportunity to do much good, — just what would suit you. It is very difficult to put it impartially. You see it would be glorious to have a musician like you amongst us, giving his best work to Germany; but it seems so selfish to press you. Yet not to press you is decidedly too unselfish. Would it not be best for you to come over and look into the whole matter yourself? In a week you would get a clear insight into everything, — town, society, and orchestra; could make your own conditions, or take theirs into consideration, — in a word, you could thoroughly sift the matter. Could n't you manage that? It would be a great gain if only for the present you did not send an absolute refusal. Do write to me soon about it, for it touches me very much.

Thanks for so kindly giving me the outlines of your new Concerto; but now I am ever so desirous to know the whole. Where is it going to be published? If not here, I hope you will send me over a copy soon. How I should like to play a manuscript of yours; that would be a real treat!

I have been rather lazy of late. From the measles I dropped straight into so much conducting that I could scarcely do anything else, save take an occasional rest. Still, I have composed a new Sonata for the piano and violoncello and three violin Quartets, which are shortly to appear. As soon as these four things are out I shall send them to you, and hope you will give me your candid opinion; but mind you criticise, and tell me what should have been otherwise, and what I ought to have done better. You are getting too indulgent and too kindly appreciative of my work. Enough for to-day; best love to wife and children. Ever remain the true friends that you are, and write soon to

Yours,

FELIX MENDELSSOHN BARTHOLDY.

I forgot to ask another favor of you. F. David, the leader of our orchestra, intends going to London next March, and wishes to play in public, if possible at the Philharmonic. Can you and will you help him to that end? I promised to ask you; and as he is a most excellent player, one of the very best we have in Germany, and as, besides, his compositions will give you pleasure, — for they are effective and brilliant, and yet well conceived and worked out, — and as he is also my very dear friend, I trust you may help him and oblige me.

LEIPZIG, Jan. 13, 1839.

MY DEAR FRIEND, — I write to-day to ask two favors of you. You once kindly offered to interest yourself on behalf of my compositions in England, and to use your influence to place them more advantageously than I could (or than they deserve). I should never have thought of accepting that kind offer, were it not for a particular case in which I cannot help asking for your assistance. The Overture for two performers which I forward to you was to have appeared simultaneously at Simrock's, in Bonn, and at Mori's, in London; the date fixed for publication was approaching, when, the day before yesterday, I got a letter from Mori, in which he expresses himself in his usual curious way, — so much so, that it makes it impossible for me to send him the piece. Now, I should be much vexed if this were to prevent its publication in England, and so I write to ask whether you can put it into the hands of some other English firm, not Mori; I do not much mind on what terms. When you look it over you will see that it is a former work numbered "Op. 24," written originally for wind instruments. I wanted it published because I thought it would give some people pleasure, and because it is easy and there are parts in it I like. If you find you can oblige me, please have it called "Duet for Two Performers" (not Overture), and put on the titlepage "Arranged from Op. 24." I must ask you, too, to let me hear from you as soon as possible, as I have written to Bonn to stop the publication till I can receive and forward your answer (on account of the title). Pardon my troubling you. It really does seem rather strong, my coming to you with such a request, but you know it is your own fault if I treat you so unceremoniously. I should prefer not to have Novello for the publisher, but to Mori on no account would I give it. Rather than that, it should not appear in England at all: not that I am at all angry with him; he is too peculiar, and for all that he still remains what he was, "My dear Sir."

My second request is in reference to David, about whom I wrote in my last long letter; an answer would much oblige him. He has written to his sister Mrs. Dulcken, asking whether she advises him to go to London in March for six or eight weeks, whether he would get an opportunity of playing his new Concerto at the Philharmonic, and what she thinks of his prospects, etc. But to this he has had no answer as yet. I had asked you to use your influence with the Directors of the Philharmonic, his talent being really remarkable both as regards his playing and his compositions; and in addition he is my very dear friend, and I feel you will be happy to know such a genuine German musician. As the time is approaching and he would have some preparations to make, I should be much obliged if you would give him a few words on the subject. Besides which I should much like a series of answers to my long letter, especially in reference to the Weimar plan. But no more bothering to-day; there has been quite enough of it in this letter. Give the kindest of messages from me to your wife, and ditto special ones from Cécile; love to the children, and an extra piece of pudding to Felix.

Do you know, I have been wishing and planning

to go to London for four weeks in April (in May I must be back on the Rhine). It would be a very foolish thing to do, but none the less delightful; and how well I could bring my wife! As I say, I have the greatest desire, but I am afraid that that is all it will come to. Now, good-by! I wrote a dreadfully long letter to Klingemann, and he answered in quite a little tiny one; but give him my best love all the same.

Yours,

FELIX MENDELSSOHN BARTHOLDY.

On the 29th of January, 1839, Moscheles writes:

"Herewith you receive the youngest child of my fancies, my 'Concerto Pastorale.' It has not yet seen the light of the musical world, and it is still a question whether it is destined to take a place in the goodly company of similar productions. So, in the mean while, I leave it under your kind care; in your hands it is bound to thrive."

Moscheles sold the copyright of Mendelssohn's Op. 24, mentioned in the preceding letter, to Messrs. Addison & Beale for twenty guineas. He says he has taken the liberty of altering some notes in the arrangement, so that nothing should stand in the way of its becoming popular with the young ladies.

David played his new Concerto at the Philharmonic on the 18th of March, and met with the most brilliant success. There, as in other concerts and musical gatherings, the purity of his style and his masterly execution were warmly appreciated.

All that Mendelssohn had written about his personal and artistic qualities was fully endorsed by Moscheles and his circle of friends. He soon became a favorite in Chester Place; and the foundation was laid for that friendship which was firmly cemented in later years, when he and Moscheles were colleagues at the Leipzig Conservatorio for nearly a quarter of a century.

LEIPZIG, Feb. 27, 1839.

MY DEAR FRIEND,— . . . Your kind letter of the 18th crossed mine on the road, and told me the disagreeable tale of the measles. How trying for all of you, especially for your dear wife! And yet it is better to go through it in your early days than to wait till you are a sedate and sober married couple like ourselves, who ought to be educating their children and conducting Oratorios, and have to lie in bed instead. However, I am thankful to say that we are out of the wood, and out of the maze of concerts too, and I 'm at my own work again, and there I always feel like a fish in the water.

But now comes the letter with the "Concerto Pastorale" (hear, hear!).[1]

The bells of the above church are just ringing: F sharp, G sharp, D sharp, and D sharp, F sharp, G sharp.

[1] See Illustration, No. 24.

19. Fac-simile from Letter of Feb. 27, 1839. (See page 182.)

My dear Moscheles, let me thank you a thousand times for being so good and kind to me, and for the great pleasure you give me by intrusting your work to me. I hardly know what to thank you most for; I think, for sending it at all. But then there is your letting me have the manuscript, and then, again, all the enjoyment I derive from it. Since it came, not a day has passed without my playing it two or three times running, and each time with increased pleasure. I am quite aware I must hear it with orchestra before I can take it in completely, and that will be to-morrow fortnight at the concert for the benefit of the Orchestra Pension Fund. We always keep a choice morsel for that occasion; so, directly I heard of it, I announced the "Concerto Pastorale," and the news was received with enthusiastic cheers. Now, I have to study desperately to get it up by that time, for it is as difficult as six others put together; and what is more, the difficulties must not be noticeable, it must all sound as fresh and light and airy as if everything went by itself. So that is what I am grinding at. So far it goes wretchedly: the end of the Adagio is specially troublesome, and won't come out at all as it should; and that most delightful two-part Dance-subject sounds as if the girl were dancing on three legs and her young man on one, — not quite your intention, I presume. At the beginning, too, I sometimes hit C in the bass and then for a change G in the treble, and that would scarcely edify you. With all this, I am hopeful; for everything lies so conveniently for the fingers, that it is their fault if it does not come right, and they have really improved since the day before yesterday, and I do think I know how it ought to be played, and that is the great thing. How delightful that unexpected introduction of the bagpipes and the tender flute at the end of the Adagio, and the 3-8 time coolly stepping in! In fact, thanks and thanks again. I should not stop if I were n't obliged to; but here comes No. 3, my Overture in C major, for which you found the right place with the right men (Cramer & Addison). I am quite ashamed of myself for having troubled you, but grateful too, and glad, for your managing all so well; that dedication to Miss Stone is a trump card, and then your writing to Simrock yourself. It is really too much kindness, my dear Moscheles; believe me, I thoroughly appreciate it, and feel deeply how much I am indebted to you.

You get this letter through David, who leaves for London with Bennett the day after to-morrow. Let me most warmly recommend him to you. He is as sympathetic, straightforward, and honest a man as ever was, a first-rate artist, and one of the few who love Art for its own sake, come what may. Please give him a kind reception, — he deserves it, — and assist him with your advice. Besides, if you wish to hear all about me and mine, nobody can better give you chapter and verse than he. We meet daily. I seldom make music without him, and what I compose he generally hears first. I wish you would let him play some of my new Quatuors to you; there are one or two amongst them I am pleased with myself, and I should like to know that I am right, and that you too are satisfied with them.

Chappell's Opera is as yet in the clouds. He was here, and took back various messages from me to Planché (and others); that is two months ago, and I have not had a syllable from him. I suggested some alterations in the text, which he approved of, and promised to submit to Planché; in the mean while nothing can be done.

I have composed several Songs, and have begun a Psalm and a new pianoforte Trio. Think of that old duet for Clarinet and Corno di Bassetto coming to the surface again! Dear me! what an old sin of mine that is, — with perhaps some touches of virtue, if I recollect right! It may be the one in D flat or that in A flat major; for I wrote two for the Bärmanns, and they played them beautifully and *con amore*. Well, I thought these old pieces were dead and buried, and now they suddenly turn up again at Moritz Schlesinger's. Not much to boast of, — this reappearance in his salons, from all I hear; but I suppose the old Duets are doomed to haunt the place in punishment of their sins.

Dreyschock is a young pianist from Prague, who must have practised like mad for several years, thus acquiring remarkable technical qualities and incredible powers of endurance, as for instance in his octave passages; but he is quite devoid of taste and musical culture. He plays some pieces so admirably that you fancy yourself in presence of a great artist, but immediately afterwards something else so poorly that you have to change your mind. The question is, Will he improve? Such as he is, he won't go far; but he has fine means at his disposal, if he will only use them; and I hope and trust he may.

If in that performance of my Psalm at the Academy, they got into trouble with the Quintet it is lucky I was not there; for that is my favorite movement, and false notes make me savage.

Our concert season will close on the 21st instead of the 15th of March, as intended; and that obliges me, much to my regret, to abandon the idea of going to England this spring. I have to be in Düsseldorf early in May, at Whitsuntide, to conduct the Festival; so I must once more postpone the pleasure of introducing my wife to you and yours. Afterwards I shall probably spend a few months on the Rhine and then return here. What are your plans for the summer?

Another request: Let Cramer & Addison (or rather Addison & Beale) know that I will draw the money for the Overture about the middle of May. I would not trouble you, but they have to be advised in advance. Really my whole letter is made up of nothing but so many requests and so many thanks!

I wish the devil himself (or, for a change, ten thousand of them) would take the English custom of putting everything into the papers. Now, I am supposed to have written to the Philharmonic that I know of no German singer to compare with Miss Novello or Miss Shaw; the story is making the rounds of the German papers, the journalists repeating it *a piacere*. You can just fancy what a precious darling the German singers think me under the circumstances; and all that, when I never wrote anything of the kind. And now, my paper is full; so good-by! Take my thanks, preserve me your friendship, and — one more request — write soon; your letters do make me so happy. Kindest remembrances from self and wife to you and your wife, and may she ever remain the true and kind friend she is! Love to the children.

Yours,

FELIX MENDELSSOHN BARTHOLDY.

LEIPZIG, April 4, 1839.

MY DEAR FRIEND, — How happy I was to get your "Concerto Pastorale," you know by my last letter. If I did not write about it again, it was because, though I had played it and got acquainted with it to a certain extent, I had yet many technical difficulties to master, and much more to study, before I could arrive at a free enjoyment of the work. And so it remained until I rehearsed it with orchestra, when for the first time I heard it properly, and began to understand it.

Since then it has, if possible, grown still dearer to me; and I am sure it will become one of my favorites amongst your works. Every time I play it I like it better and better. We had two regular orchestral rehearsals, repeating the whole piece, as well as single movements. And so, when the evening came, it went very well and correctly, and you would have been satisfied, — that is, with the orchestra, not with me, I am afraid; for that night I was the victim of a dreadful cold (which, by the way, I have not got rid of yet), and at one time — it was just at the beginning of the Solo in the Adagio — a spasmodic fit of coughing threatened to bring me to a dead stop. So my playing was not as spirited as I should have liked it to be; but I got through it pretty correctly, excepting the octave passage, — some parts coming out better than they had ever done whilst I was studying them. The public applauded tremendously, and entered into the spirit of the work with more sympathy and feeling than I should have given them credit for. You know I am not generally an admirer of the public; but this time they did try to get at the meaning of the piece, and some of them had really arrived at a right conclusion and understanding. A desire was expressed on all sides to hear it again. But unluckily, this is just the end of our concert season; and now comes the annual fair, and our unmusical time, and I shall not play again here till next autumn. How long can I keep the parts? When will you want them in London?

And now, my dear friend, once more a thousand thanks for the pleasure you have given us all; thanks for the fine composition you have contributed to our concerts; thanks in particular for having intrusted it to me.

We recently played a most remarkable and interesting Symphony by Franz Schubert. It is without doubt one of the best works we have lately heard. Throughout bright, fascinating, and original, it stands quite at the head of his instrumental works. Spohr's Symphony, which we performed before, I suppose you will give in the Philharmonic. Lachner's I liked but little; the others liked it less. David can tell you all about these. I have written a new Theatre-Overture[1] that has been quite a source of pleasure to me; also a Psalm (again *vide* David); some Songs without words (according to the "Hegira" of David), some with words; and now a Trio in D, and a Symphony in B, of which I will tell you more when they are finished.

Good-by, etc.,

FELIX MENDELSSOHN BARTHOLDY.

In the following lines Moscheles introduces the well-known writer and musical critic. Henry F. Chorley: —

LONDON, Aug. 17, 1839.

MY DEAR FRIEND, — The bearer of these lines, Henry F. Chorley, is an excellent and highly culti-

[1] Overture to "Ruy Blas."

vated young man; he is on the staff of the "Athenæum," and has made himself a name as an author and as an enthusiastic lover of music, not only appreciating what is good, but discriminating between the good and the trivial. Above all, he has, for a long time past, been welcome at my house as a true and genial friend. He has an intimate acquaintance and full sympathy with you and your work. In a very exhaustive article published in the "Quarterly Review," he has characteristically portrayed the most eminent pianists and composers; the sketch he draws of you there, is worthy of his subject.

LEIPZIG, Nov. 30, 1839.

MY DEAR FRIEND, — I cannot understand why I so seldom write to you; for I thoroughly enjoy it when I do, and only wonder why I did not settle down to it before. What with the many visitors, and all kinds of business, — requests and behests that would really come more appropriately ten years hence than now, when I do not feel at all like settling down to a life of business, — I lose my head, and just do everything excepting that which gives me pleasure and which I ought to do. Well, you must be indulgent. Your letters make me happy for days to come, and I read them over and over again, and am grateful for your never-failing friendship and kindness. And how wonderful it all seems when I think of those days in Berlin when I first saw you, and you stretched out the hand of kindly encouragement to me, whilst the *dii minorum gentium* and all manner of little imps were making most horrible faces at me; and when I remember how, through all changes, you have never varied in your friendship and forbearance, and are now just what you were then, and how, after all, I am much the same as I was! To be sure, since then we have both become *pater-familias.* By this time your daughter must be styled "Miss," whereas mine only came into the world on the 2d of October; and whilst your boy is already playing his scales, mine is playing at nothing at all, not even at horse.

Your Paris letter gave me much pleasure, although what it describes is anything but pleasant. What a curious state of things seems to prevail there! To say the truth, I never felt very sympathetically disposed towards it; and all I have lately heard, through you and others, does not tend to improve my opinion. Vanity and outward show nowhere seem to play so prominent a part; and the fact that people do not pose only for stars, decorations, and stiff neckties, but for high art, and for souls replete with enthusiasm, does not mend matters. When I read your description of the *soirée* at Kalkbrenner's, I see and hear it all. That anxiety to shine at the pianoforte, that greed for a poor little round of applause, the shallowness that underlies it all and is as pretentious as if such petty exhibitions were events of world-wide importance! To read about it is more than enough for me. After all, I prefer the German Philistine, with his nightcap and tobacco; although I am not the one to stand up in his defence, especially since the events in Hanover, which I followed with great interest, and which, I am sorry to say, do not reflect much credit on the German fatherland. So, on the whole, there is not much to be proud of on either side; and one cannot help being doubly grateful for that Art which has a life of its own far away from everything, — a solitude to which we can fly and be happy.

And now I want to know what you are writing. Chorley told me so much about some new "Studies;" when shall I get to see and play them? And so you are really going to dedicate your "Concerto Pastorale" to me? I don't know how to set about telling you what pleasure it gives me, and how honored I feel to have my name associated with one of your works. Let me confess to you that you have fulfilled a long-standing wish of mine; for the C minor Capriccio appeared in Germany without my name, and now I am doubly happy to be identified with so important a work of yours. I will at once set to practising again, so as to do it more justice. It is curious how often I look through heaps of new music without feeling any inclination to practise, and then when I come across a piece that is really good, one that I must play, and can play with pleasure, I feel as if I had suddenly found a new set of fingers (some training they require, to be sure).

I want to write a new Concerto, but so far it is swimming about in my head in a shapeless condition. A new Oratorio, too, I have begun; but how it 's to end, and what is to come in the middle, Heaven only knows. My Trio I should so like to show you; it has grown quite dear to me, and I am confident there are things in it you would be satisfied with. Could I but bring you over here for a day or two, and play it to you, and have your criticisms and your advice as to what I should alter and what I might do better another time, then there would be a chance of my learning something; but at a distance, and by letter, it is n't half the same thing. The publishers are pressing me to let them have it, and I want to do so; I only wish I could just once play it to you before.

As for the Opera for Chappell, I am sorry to say it is as much in the clouds as ever: the old trouble about the libretto! What is the use of beginning so important a work, with the absolute conviction that I could not make anything decent of it? Chorley, who has promised me his assistance, is a truly good fellow, for whose acquaintance I owe you many thanks; one seldom meets a man so highly cultivated, and at the same time so simple and natural. Remember me very kindly to him. I mean to write to him, and should have done so already if I did not feel the awkwardness of using that language which he writes so delightfully, and which I somewhat ill-treat. He seems to have been much pleased with our concerts; and in fact we might really do something grand if there were just a little more money to spend. That blessed money pulls us up at every step, and we don't get on half as well as we should like to. On the one hand stand the Philistines who believe that Leipzig is Paris, and everything perfection, and that if our musicians were not starved it would no longer be Leipzig; on the other hand stand the musicians, — or rather they *run* as soon as they see a chance, and I even back them up with letters to help them out of their misery. A pretty business it would have been if you had kept our David! I should once for all have stuck in the mud, and should never have got on to decent orchestra legs again. His violin alone is worth ten good ones; and with that he is such a musician! Besides, really now, he leads quite an agreeable life here, and is petted and beloved by the public. No, him we positively cannot spare. Miss Meerti, who sends her kind regards, has won golden opinions here. She has a sympathetic and beautiful voice, and is a nice, amiable girl besides; she is quite a favorite with us, and is now going to Dresden, where she is invited to sing at Court.

I will make this letter a double one, and will enclose an old German ballad, in order to keep up the practice of sending a song to your wife. Excuse the postage.

Acting on your advice, I sent the "Study" to Schlesinger, though I cannot bear the fellow. He and Fétis make a pair, from whom may the gods preserve those they love! But then, to be sure, your name counterbalances a thousand or so of their calibre; and whatever you do, or wherever you go, there I follow with pleasure. I did not answer Schlesinger's letter of last summer, because he had been rather too aggravating, and I wanted to leave him in peace, so that he might leave me in peace. However, thanks to your letter, I am now more mildly disposed; and after all, one publisher is as good as another. But I must say I do not think I shall ever get on well with this one. I declined to give anything to Pott in furtherance of his scheme; nor would you have done so, had you known all their doings and dealings in Germany with regard to monuments. They speculate on the names of great men in order to make themselves great names; they do a deal of trumpeting in the papers, and treat us to ever so much bad music with the real trumpets. If they will honor Handel in Halle, Mozart in Frankfurt and Salzburg, and Beethoven in Bonn, by founding good orchestras and performing their works properly and intelligently, I am their man. But I don't care for their stones and blocks as long as their orchestras are only stumbling-blocks; nor for their Conservatorios in which there is nothing worth conserving. My present hobby is the improvement of our poor orchestra. After no end of letter-writing, soliciting, and importuning, I have succeeded in getting their salaries raised by five hundred thalers; and before I leave them I mean to get them double that amount. If that is granted, I won't mind their setting a monument to Sebastian Bach in front of the Saint Thomas school; but first, mind you, the grant. You see I am a regular small-beer Leipziger. But really you would be touched if you could see and hear for yourself how my good fellows put heart and soul into their work, and strive to do their best.

I am very glad you improved your acquaintance and friendship with Chopin. He is certainly the most gifted of them all, and his playing has real charm. They say Liszt is coming here, and I should be very glad; for notwithstanding his unpalatable contributions to the papers, I am fully impressed both by his playing and by his striking personality. Berlioz's programme, that you send me, is a very silly production. I wish I could see any pluck or originality in it, but to me it seems simply vapid and insipid. Has not Onslow written anything new? And old Cherubini? There is a man for you! I have got his "Abencerrages," and am again and again enjoying his sparkling fire, his clever and unexpected transitions, and the neatness and grace with which he writes. I am truly grateful to the fine old gentleman. It is all so free, so bold and bright.

Now I must end, my dear, dear friend. I have been jumbling everything together, and chatting

20. "Des Hirten Winterlied." In Letter of Nov. 18, 1840, to Mrs. Moscheles.
(See page 217.)

away as if I were sitting next to you by the piano. Would it were so! But for that I may have to wait some time; so, meanwhile, write to me and let me know what you are doing and what composing; and above all, tell me that you are my friend, as I am yours,

FELIX MENDELSSOHN BARTHOLDY.

LEIPZIG, March 21, 1840.
Beginning of Spring.

MY DEAR FRIEND, — Those kind letters of yours and your wife's came yesterday, and a most agreeable surprise they were. A thousand thanks. You cannot imagine how refreshing it is to me to get a letter from you. Besides all that is new and interesting in it, there is so much that comes straight from the heart, so much that is thoroughly Moscheles, that I quite fancy I hear you. And, do you know, one of the invigorating effects of your letters is the desire they give me to go to England, whereas, in truth, I fight rather shy of the journey. I don't know how it is, but when I read your letter urging me to go to Birmingham, I am seized with the desire to be off. There is my wife, too, who is in favor of the journey, and who, this time, would like to accompany me; and that sets me to thinking that we might do worse than bring our wives together, and let them become friends; and then — and then — I long for the steamer and for the perfume of British coal, and I put in the daintiest touches to complete the pleasant picture. I wonder whether it is to be realized.

What you tell me about the Philharmonic and Lord Burghersh, I must say, does not particularly attract me; that the society should be losing ground, as you say, I most sincerely regret. It was so flourishing when I knew it, and had such a halo of glory round it, that I could not believe the evil I hear of it on all sides; but since you confirm such reports, they must be true.

Your remarks on Spohr's C minor Symphony, I indorse word for word; and without knowing his historical Symphony, one feels how correct and fair your analysis of it must be, just as one can judge of the likeness of a portrait without knowing the subject.[1] But what an unlucky idea the whole thing is! After all, a joke is out of place in a serious orchestra. This leads me to a request that I meant to make long ago. Would you not let us have your own Symphony in C[2] for one of our concerts? I am sure it would be appreciated on all sides, and why should you withhold such a work from the public? For this winter it would be too late, as our last concert takes place on Thursday; but it might come as an opening feature of the concert season next autumn, if you are agreeable.

We have had an interesting musical time of it,

[1] The letter alluded to is not amongst the copies of Moscheles's letters in the possession of the editor.

[2] Op. 81.

this winter: Dreyschock, Prume, Madame Pleyel, Hiller, Ernst, and now, to wind up, Liszt. Our Subscription Concerts and the six Quartet evenings were more crowded than ever; and with their close the time has come when one longs for home music and no concerts. Liszt has been here for the last six days. He has given one concert, and announces another for next Tuesday; after which he goes to Dresden and to Paris, where he means to play; afterwards to London for the season, and then to Russia to spend the winter. His playing, which is quite masterly, and his subtle musical feeling, that finds its way to the very tips of his fingers, truly delighted me. His rapidity and suppleness, above all, his playing at sight, his memory, and his thorough musical insight, are qualities quite unique in their way, and that I have never seen surpassed. With all that, you find in him, when once you have penetrated beneath the surface of modern French polish, a good fellow and a true artist, whom you can't help liking even if you disagree with him. The only thing that he seems to me to want is true talent for composition, I mean really original ideas. The things he played to me struck me as very incomplete, even when judged from his own point of view, which, to my mind, is not the right one. And, if I am not mistaken, that explains why Thalberg would meet with more success in many places, — England, for instance. He, in his way, is just perfect; he plays the pieces he has mastered, and there he stops: whereas Liszt's whole performance is as unpremeditated, as wild and impetuous, as you would expect of a genius; but then I miss those genuinely original ideas which I naturally expect from a genius. A mere pianist he is not, nor does he give himself out as such; and that perhaps makes him appear less perfect than others whose talent cannot be compared with his. We are together the greater part of the day, and seem to be mutually attracted. His appreciation of you, and the cordial way in which he expresses it, have drawn me still nearer to him. It is a pity that he should be saddled with a manager and a secretary who, between them, succeeded in so thoroughly mismanaging things that the public were furious, and we had the greatest trouble to smooth matters to some extent for the second concert. The advertisements and subsequent modifications, the prices and the programme, — in fact, everything that Liszt himself did not do was objectionable; and consequently the mildest of Leipzigers were in a rage. By this time, however, they seem to have calmed down again.

A thousand thanks for your kind offer about my Trio. I need not trouble you again about its publication, as it is to appear at Ewer & Co.'s; but your offer to look through the proof-sheets is too tempting to refuse, however indiscreet my acceptance may be. So I have told Ewer to send you the proofs, and am sincerely obliged to you.

They asked me for an arrangement for the flute instead of the violin, and I suggested that they should publish only the Andante and Scherzo in this form, under the title "Andante et Rondo (tiré de l'œuvre 49," etc.); because the first and last movements appear too heavy and substantial for such an arrangement. However, I have left the decision in their hands. What do you advise? I have told them to consult you on any question which might arise. That, too, you must excuse; but, above all, let me soon know what you think of the work itself.

You know how highly I value your remarks, and how much at all times I learn from them. For that self-same reason I wish I could show you a new Psalm I have just written, and a Symphony I have begun. Well, perhaps that may be next autumn.

And now good-by. Yours ever,

FELIX MENDELSSOHN BARTHOLDY.

LEIPZIG, July 2, 1840.

DEAR MRS. MOSCHELES,—I should have thanked you for your kind and friendly letter by return of post, had I been able to say anything certain about my visit to England. But that is so far impossible. What with constant conducting and preparing for public performances, I have lately been so knocked up that the doctor seriously advises me to take a few months' rest before the beginning of our busy season in October. You can fancy that I shall only do so if necessity compels me; so one day I am quite resolved to go to England, and the next, I feel obliged to abandon the idea. To-day I leave for Mecklenburg, where, for some time past, I have promised to conduct a festival; and until we see what effect that has on my health, I cannot make any further plans. Should I, after that, feel strong enough to stand the fatigue of an English music festival, nothing shall detain me, and come I will. I shall let you know the when as soon as I can clearly see my way out of the ifs and buts. . . .

And now farewell to you and yours; and to Moscheles, especially, the most cordial and hearty messages I can think of.

Yours,

FELIX MENDELSSOHN BARTHOLDY.

LEIPZIG, Aug. 8, 1840.

DEAR MRS. MOSCHELES, — Hurrah! I'm coming. I cannot give you a date; for if I bring my wife[1] (as I hope and trust to do), I shall start in about a fortnight, whereas, if I come alone, I shall be in London on the 8th of September, remain for the Festival, and return immediately after it. In the latter case I should have to abandon the long-cherished plan of introducing my wife to the coun-

[1] After all, Mrs. Mendelssohn was prevented from going to England.

try of my predilection and the dear friends I have there.

I fully rely upon your remaining in England and going to Birmingham as you promised. What a delightful trip we could make of it! What a pleasure to see Moscheles again, and to hear him! And then, all his new compositions which I shall really get to know and enjoy, whereas hitherto I have had to be satisfied with a kind of a sort of a description, or half a bar here and there doled out to me by some friend just fresh from London. We'll have a regular feast of music. I, for one, am hungrier and thirstier for it than ever. And my godson, and the two charming young ladies, now grown to the dignity of real "misses,"—I shall have to renew my friendship with them, or rather take it up where we left it; and possibly Emily may have some dim recollection of former pianoforte lessons, and Serena of certain carnations. I shall expect my godson to remember having met me at St. Pancras Church,[1] and to call me by my name. Of myself I can only say, you will find me a hopeless case. Whatever talent I might have shown for speaking the English language or behaving like a gentleman, has been lost in the atmosphere of German petty provincialism. In some things you will find me unchanged, but won't it annoy you all the more that I have not improved? Well, all that crosses my mind occasion-

[1] St. Pancras was the church at which Mendelssohn stood godfather to Felix Moscheles.

ally; but then I console myself with the thought that you will be pleased to see an old friend, whether he is improved or not, cleverer or less clever, and will give him, as of old, your friendship and your indulgence. How glad that friend, on *his* part, is at the idea of soon finding himself in your family again, it needs no words to assure you. May we meet in health and happiness, and may you be as kindly disposed as ever to

Yours,

FELIX MENDELSSOHN BARTHOLDY.

On the 18th of September Mendelssohn arrived in London. Mrs. Moscheles writes of him to her relatives in Hamburg: —

"Our dear Mendelssohn — I cannot call him otherwise — arrived at four o'clock, was with us at seven, just the same warm and genial friend as of old; bright, cordial, and hearty, — in a word, the type of a true man. Klingemann and Chorley joined him here at dinner; and in the evening Felix junior had such a tremendous romp with his godfather, that the whole house shook. One can scarcely realize that the man who was presently improvising in his grandest style, was the same as the Felix senior, the king of games and romps."

On the 20th of September Mendelssohn and Moscheles went to Birmingham. From there the latter writes: —

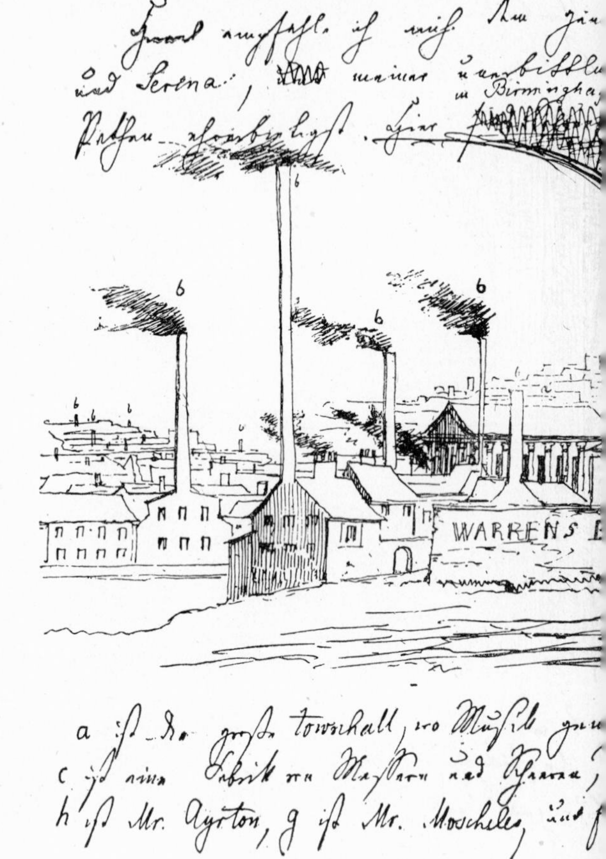

21. Birmingham. From a Pen Dra

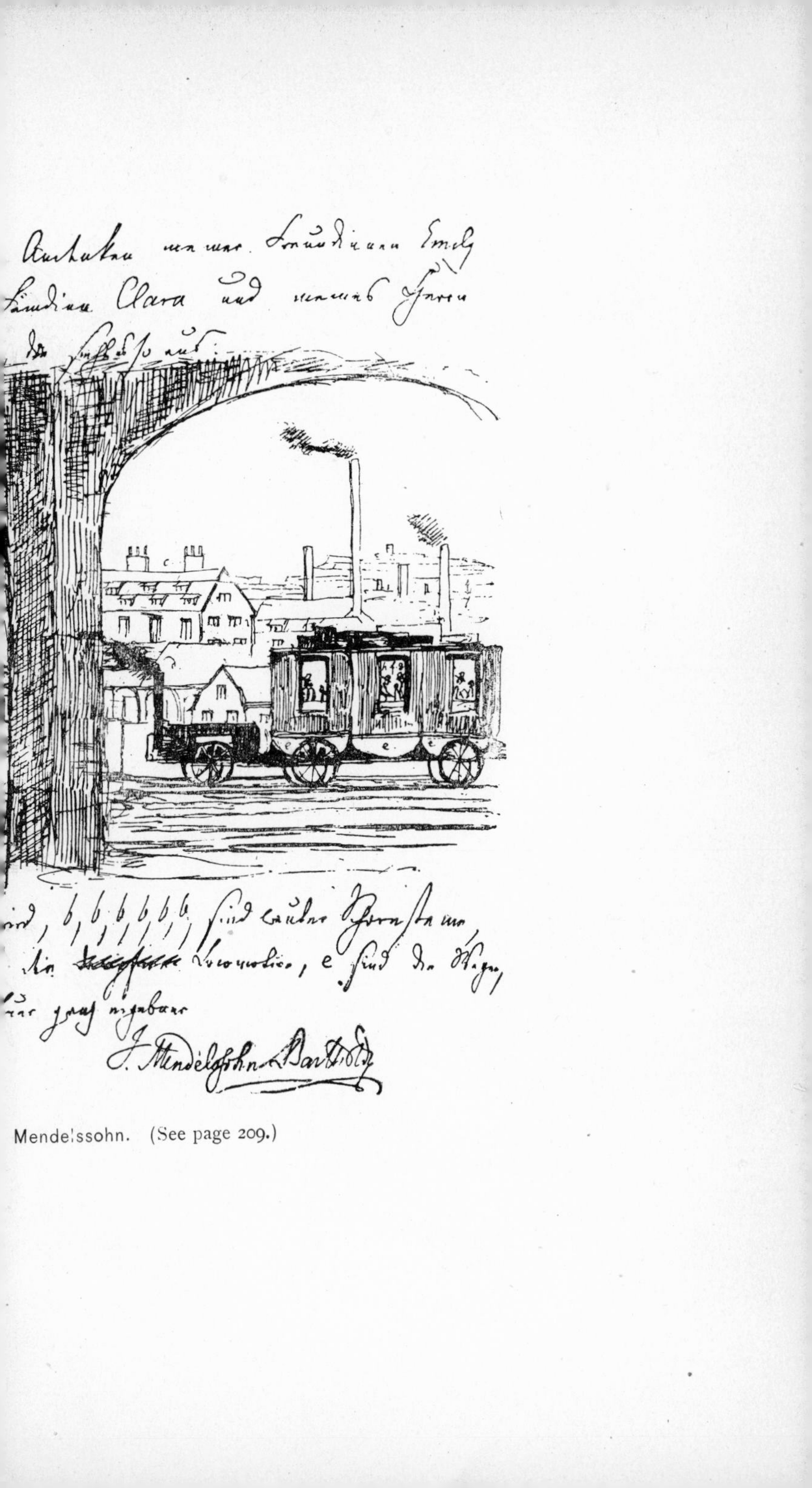

Mendelssohn. (See page 209.)

"Whilst all Birmingham was congratulating itself on having the heaven-born composer within its walls, and on the privilege of hearing him conduct his latest work, he, in the midst of a thousand duties, found leisure to make for the children a pen-and-ink sketch of the city, with its town hall, its houses, smoky chimneys, and all."[1]

Further on Moscheles describes the performance of Mendelssohn's "Hymn of Praise," and ends with the words: —

"A powerful Fugue next breaks in triumphantly, the majestic tone of the organ resounds, and a double set of kettledrums marks the rhythm, much as a throbbing pulse marks the course of the life-blood through a man's veins. Then follows a Chorale of such dignity, that involuntarily the whole audience rose from their seats as is usually done only during the 'Hallelujah.' Afterwards, when the hall was emptied, he played for three quarters of an hour on the organ, before a small circle of friends, just as if he had neither been hearing nor conducting music, but as if his day's work was only then beginning."

After a short stay in London, Mendelssohn, Moscheles, and Chorley started together for Leipzig. On the eve of his departure Mendelssohn made a

[1] See Illustration, No. 21.

pen-and-ink sketch in Mrs. Moscheles's album, full of pleasant allusions to their stay in Birmingham. On the left he draws the Stork Hotel, in which they had taken up their quarters; and next to it a pair of scissors which he had presented to Mrs. Moscheles, and which are drawn stalking vaingloriously along and towering over the Town Hall, of Festival memories. Then comes the Bread-and-Butter Pudding, his favorite dish, the recipe of which he was carrying home with him.

Further on, the cravat which Mrs. Moscheles had given him. He was in the habit of protesting that he had never been able to master the art of adjusting his cravat, and that not until Mrs. Moscheles pronounced the magic words, "Pin it up," was a flood of light thrown on the subject. Above the cravat the steamer stands in readiness for the morrow; below, the mail-coach and the luggage, — amongst the latter, a certain umbrella belonging to Moscheles, which Mendelssohn had unfortunately lost, is conspicuous.[1]

They started on the 3d of October; and their adventures by sea and land are recorded in a humorous letter penned by the trio of friends, Mendelssohn adding a little sketch of the pitching boat he had every reason to remember.[2]

During his ten days' stay in Leipzig, Moscheles writes frequent letters to his wife. The following note of invitation Mendelssohn enclosed in one of them: —

[1] See Illustration, No. 22. [2] See Illustration, No. 23.

22. An Album Sketch by Mendelssohn. (See page 210.)

MRS. MENDELSSOHN

is respectfully invited to a musical evening party to be given on Monday, the [illegible] of October, at 6 o'clock precisely, in the rooms of the Gewandhaus, by

FELIX MENDELSSOHN-BARTHOLDY.

[illegible]

It is requested that this paper be presented at the door; [illegible]

An answer is requested by return of post.

The "Musical evening party" went off in a most brilliant manner. Moscheles describes the brilliant and festive scene, and the charming way in which Mr. and Mrs. Mendelssohn received their three hundred guests. The chorus of one hundred and forty voices was most effective, and the Gewandhaus orchestra was never heard to better advantage.

After a short visit to his mother in Prague, Moscheles hurried back to London, reluctantly foregoing the pleasure he had promised himself of once more shaking hands with his friends before leaving Germany.

MRS. MOSCHELES

is respectfully invited to a musical evening party to be given on Monday, the 19th of October, at 6 o'clock precisely, in the rooms of the Gewandhaus, by

FELIX MENDELSSOHN BARTHOLDY,

there to hear his 42d Psalm, with Orchestra, his Overture to "Fingal's Cave," and Moscheles's Overture to "Joan of Arc." Moscheles, the "Father of Pianists" (as Fink calls him in the "Musical Gazette"), will play his G minor Concerto, as also Bach's Triple Concerto, with Madame Schumann and Dr. F. Mendelssohn Bartholdy, in addition to which he will perform some of his characteristic Studies.

It is requested that this paper be presented at the doors; should, however, this request not be complied with, Professor Moscheles will have to proceed to London in order to receive that applause which here can but be incomplete.

An answer by return of post will oblige.

The "musical evening party" turned out a most brilliant one. Moscheles describes the bright and festive scene, and the charming way in which Mr. and Mrs. Mendelssohn received their three hundred guests. The chorus of one hundred and forty voices was most effective, and the Gewandhaus orchestra was never heard to better advantage.

After a short visit to his mother in Prague, Moscheles hurried back to London, reluctantly foregoing the pleasure he had promised himself of once more shaking hands with his friends before leaving Germany.

LEIPZIG, Nov. 18, 1840.

DEAR MRS. MOSCHELES, — I fancy Moscheles once more comfortably installed by your "fireside" (this can't be expressed in German); so now I must write and send greetings, and say how often and with what heartfelt gratitude I remember our late meeting. After our parting there followed some pleasant days, which Moscheles's and Chorley's letters have long ago described to you. Now, however, that Moscheles has left us by train, and Chorley by *Schnellpost,* a quiet time has set in, with scarcely anything to describe, — for happiness itself is indescribable; and, indeed, I ought neither to form a wish nor to express a regret, when I enjoy, as I do at present, health and contentment with my wife and children, and have plenty of work to do; yet I must say we were truly sorry on receiving Moscheles's letter, definitely putting off his return to us. He had become quite a member of the family during his short stay, and as such we parted from him. He seemed to be in most friendly sympathy with my wife; such feelings are generally mutual, and I know she took to him the very first day. But when will my prophecy be fulfilled, that you too will love my Cécile, and feel at home and intimate with her? Not this next spring, I fear; and whether Moscheles is so favorably impressed with Germany that he wishes soon to repeat his visit, that too remains to be seen; but I hope he did feel

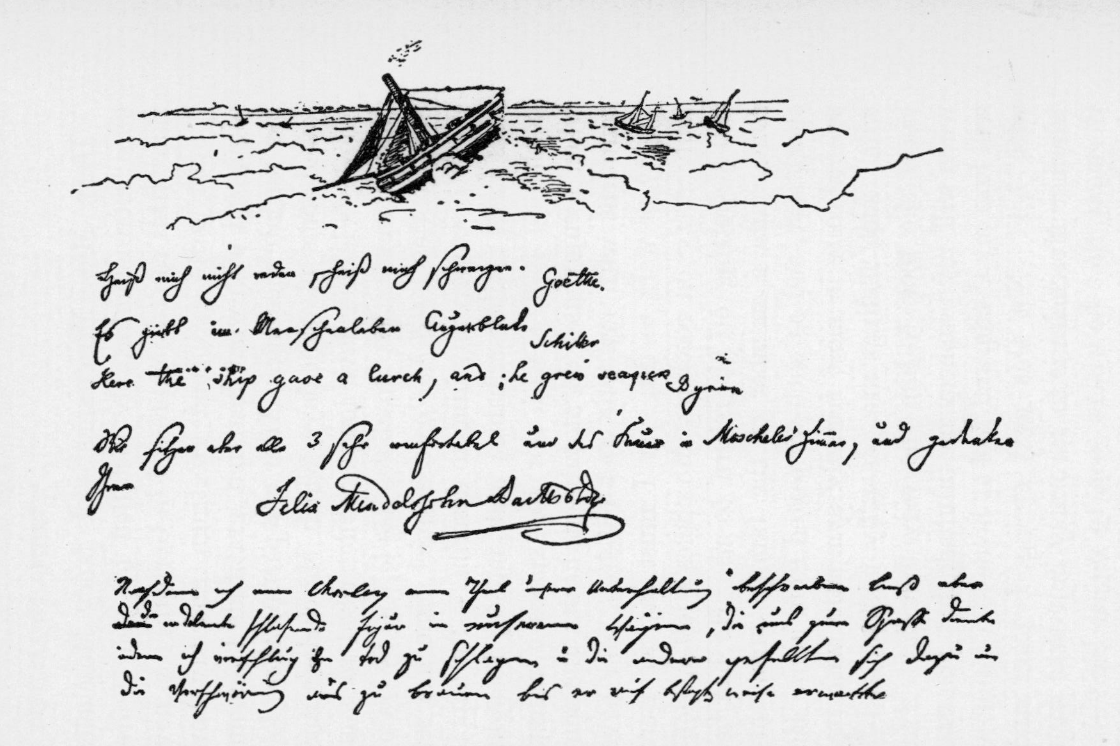

23. Fac-simile from the Joint Letter from Ostend. (See page 210; also, explanation in the List of Illustrations.)

what we all had at heart, — what every one of us would have liked to show in word and deed, if the very showing and saying had not been our weak point, though he will nowhere find it more strongly developed, — the most heartfelt reverence and love for himself and his work, and the most sincere gratitude for the immense enjoyment he has procured us. It is still our daily talk; and even little Carl[1] never passes a day without asking Papa, "How does my uncle Mosche*n*es play?" Then I try to imitate it with my fists in A flat, six-eight time as well as I can, but the result is miserable. Now comes a song.[2] . . .

I will give the pen to my wife, and only add love to the dear children, to whom pray remember me. This letter is for Moscheles too. How glad I was to hear of his successes in Prague, I need not say. I trust he thinks of us as we do of him, and that we may soon hear of his safe arrival. Farewell, dear Mrs. Moscheles.

Ever yours,

FELIX MENDELSSOHN BARTHOLDY.

LEIPZIG, March 14, 1841.

DEAR MOSCHELES, — Just as I was sitting down to answer your kindest of letters (dated the 9th inst.), in comes bright No. 2, with its graphic account of the Taylor evening, and its other capital

[1] Little Carl was Mendelssohn's eldest child. Moscheles used to amuse him by playing a tune on the piano with his fists.

[2] See Illustration, No. 20.

and vivid descriptions. David must take you my answer to both, and my very best thanks for the pleasure they have given me. He leaves to-morrow. There is no need once more to recommend him, his wife, and their little daughter to you and yours. You know and appreciate him and his art already, and are sure to contribute more than your share towards making his stay agreeable. Mind you don't get too fond of him, and keep him there altogether; we Germans could not allow that, for men and musicians of his stamp are not as thickly sown out here as you might fancy. So make as much of him as you like, but send him back well preserved afterwards.

And now to return to your two delightful letters. The first contained the enclosures from Broadley and instructions in reference to the German publication; they shall be punctually carried out. Please ask him to mention on the titlepage of the English edition that Simrock of Bonn is the German publisher. May I beg you to communicate this to him without delay? Make my excuses to him (and yourself) for not having sent the short prelude. I would gladly do so; but really, with the best will in the world, I could not write a short prelude to suit that piece without altering the whole form and giving it a pretentious coloring, which it should not have. I would rather leave it to the organist to tumble his fingers about at random, making it long or short as he likes, and as rich or poor as he can afford.

I do wish I could hear your Psalm. You know how much I should enjoy it. But how could I venture to make suggestions, or even to *think* them, when I am so full of the beauties I find in your work, and so thankful, as we all have reason to be, for what you give us in so full a measure? At any rate, you know that I, for one, feel deeply grateful for the bright products of your art; and I trust you will always let me have the new things you write, and particularly that you will not let me wait long for the Psalm and the two new "Studies."

According to your kind permission, I have put together a book of your Songs, selected from the ten you sent me through Dr. Becker. Kistner required six for a book; so I chose the following: "Stumme Liebe," by Probald; "Der Schmidt," by Uhland; "Zuversicht," by the Countess Hahn; "Das Reh," by Uhland; "Im Herbst," by Uhland; "Sakontala," by Klingemann. The keys certainly follow in the maddest of ways,—F major, B major, and so on anyhow; but I have always found that not a soul thanks you for the loveliest sequence in keys, and that it is rather a change from slow to fast, from serious to lively, that is particularly in demand. So pray excuse this fricassee of sharps and flats.

Yours,

FELIX MENDELSSOHN BARTHOLDY.

LEIPZIG, March 14, 1841.

DEAR MRS. MOSCHELES, — What a delightful letter of yours that was I received the day before yesterday, written beside the singing tea-urn, and taking me straight to Chester Place! By rights, my thanks ought to come in the shape of a song on one of these pages; but I cannot manage it to-day, and you must take these unmusical, prosaic, dry thanks for your musical, bright, poetical letter. For now, when our season is drawing to a close, you know from experience how hard-driven a man is, — and, to keep up the usual distinction, a musician into the bargain. Since January we are having an uninterrupted succession of musical doings, besides which the Leipzigers are so very sociable that at this time one is scarcely ever allowed a quiet evening at home. Our own house has become a lively centre too. Sophy Horsley has arrived, seems to feel at home with us, and is already making friends with my wife; and now we invite our friends, and they return the compliment. We speak German, French, and English, all in one breath; and all the while the orchestra is fiddling, trumpeting, and drumming every day, whilst one is expected to sit an hour and a half at supper, and sing four-part songs to a roast-beef accompaniment.

The only thing I regret in your charming letter is that you should have countenanced the strange attempts at making comparisons between Spohr and myself, or the petty cock-fights in which, for some inconceivable reason and much to my regret, we have been pitted against each other in England. I never had the slightest idea of such competition or rivalry. You may laugh at me, or possibly be vexed, at my taking up such a silly matter so seriously. But there is something serious at the bottom of it; and this pretended antagonism, imagined and started by Heaven knows whom, can in no way serve either of us, but must rather be detrimental to both. Besides, never could I appear as the opponent of a master of Spohr's standing, whose greatness is so firmly established; for, even as a boy, I had the greatest esteem for him in every respect, and, with my riper years, this feeling has in no way been weakened.

And so the Philharmonic Society seems tumbling to pieces. Oh dear! oh dear! how sad that is! It is true they have worried me a good deal of late; still I have a sort of affection for the old familiar institution, and hope they may yet conceive the brilliant idea of appointing Moscheles as sole conductor; that would be the infallible remedy to save them (see Chorley's MS. receipts).

And how are your children? Does Emily keep up her playing? Does she compose? And does Felix drop down all of a heap in his popular character of the dead man? We are all right, thank goodness! My wife has been in such good health all this time that I cannot be sufficiently thankful.

There is, however, much to manage and arrange with three little soprano singers in the house, and that is why she returns your kind messages through me. Sophy desires her very best love, and repeats it three times, emphasizing alternately each of the three words; and I say, should you ever feel inclined to write such another truly charming letter by the side of the tea-urn, so enjoyable to your distant friends, drawing them into your family circle, then think of

Yours,

FELIX MENDELSSOHN BARTHOLDY.

JUNE 15, 1841.

MY DEAR FRIEND, — How shall I thank you for those two beautiful "Studies" you sent me! I cannot tell you how much I have found in them to enjoy and to admire, and how grateful I am that you should select me as the first to send them to, in advance of the whole musical world, that takes so lively an interest in all you write. That is truly kind of you.

To tell the truth, it is the one in D minor that is my favorite, particularly in that modulation on the seventh, after the long F  , and the return to D minor, passing through C and E flat. But then there is that lively one in F major, which I love more and more each time I play it. And

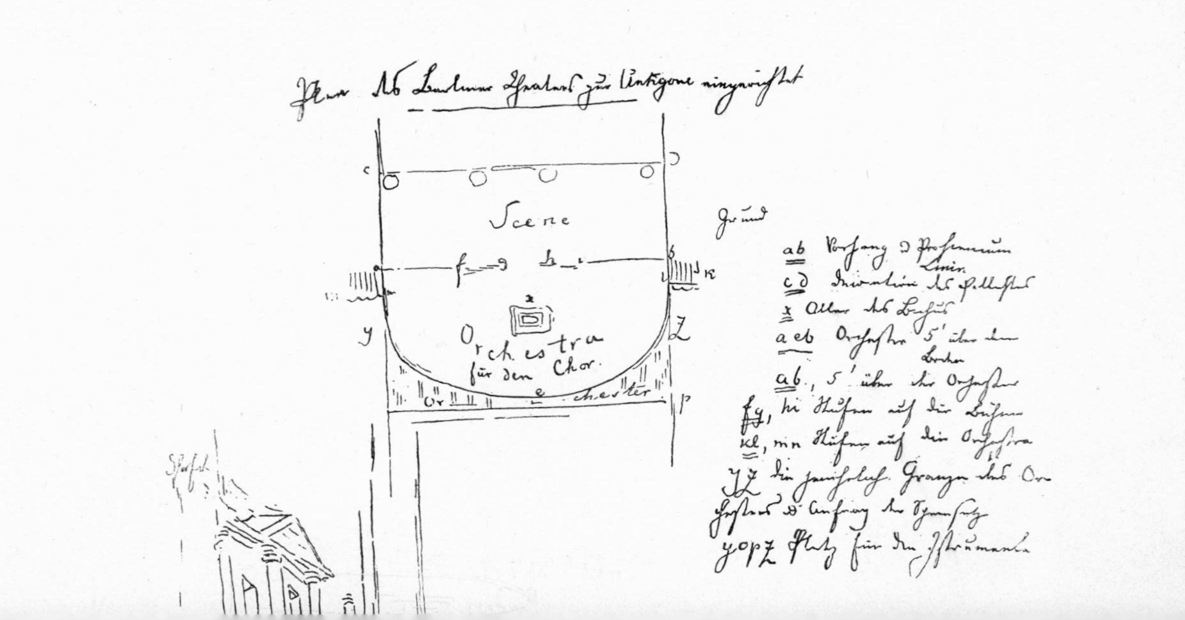
Plan des Berliner Theaters zur Antigone eingerichtet
Scene
Orchestra
für den Chor

24. Stage Arrangements at Berlin. Fac-simile of Drawing by Mendelssohn.
(See explanation in the List of Illustrations.)

finally, they are both so truly Moscheles that it is hard to choose! Well, there they are, both of them; so there is no necessity to make a choice.

Will you allow me an observation, — the only one that occurred to me? There is something in the last two bars of the D minor Study, the end of which I otherwise like so much, that sounds strange to my ear. The long rest on the seventh, and then the F in the melody (half a bar before the last) gives to that passage a melodious coloring that does not seem to me quite in keeping with the general character of the Study. I think some simpler, bolder final chord would be more in harmony with the whole. It is a trifling objection, you see, and perhaps I am altogether wrong; so excuse the liberty and set me right.

It does strut along so splendidly, that D minor Study; and I can play it pretty well already too. The one in F I cannot manage at all yet, although I have tried hard.

Your putting at the head of them the words "Without characteristic names," is, I can see, an allusion to my pert remarks in Gotha. Well, you must pardon them, as well as all others in the past, and possibly in the future. Let me thank you too, my dear friend, in my wife's name and in my own, for the dedication of your Songs. It is a kind gift we shall ever value.

You will have heard that I am going for a year to Berlin. I could not refuse, but fully intend to return at the end of the time. I would rather be here than there. To be sure, I am to rejoice in the title of Kapellmeister, to get a lot of money, and to have no special duties, either at the theatre or elsewhere,— in fact, to be quite my own master; but with all that, I don't quite like it. I shall be there in about ten days; and as soon as I can tell you more about it, you shall hear from me. Yours ever,

FELIX MENDELSSOHN BARTHOLDY.

In June, 1842, Mendelssohn once more returned to London, this time accompanied by his wife; and so at last Mrs. Moscheles had the opportunity, to which she had been looking forward so long, of making Cécile Mendelssohn's acquaintance, and of welcoming her to England. They met, as might be expected, fully disposed to indorse the bond of friendship that united their husbands. Sympathetically attracted to one another at the outset, they soon exchanged the more formal mode of address for the affectionate "Du," therein following the example of their husbands, who, years ago, had in the same way taken the pledge of brotherhood. Their friendship continued and remained unchanged until the premature death of Cécile Mendelssohn.

On the 13th of June Mendelssohn conducted his A minor Symphony for the first time in the Philharmonic. He played with Moscheles in a concert arranged by the latter for the benefit of

Canone a 3. unis.

Zu freundlicher Erinnerung beim Durchblättern dieses Buches

Felix Mendelssohn Bartholdy

London d. 11. July
1842.

25. Fac-simile from a Letter written in July, 1842.

the sufferers from the Hamburg fire, — a venture which was eminently successful, the net receipts amounting to £650. Sophocles's "Antigone" was performed in Moscheles's house, Mendelssohn being at the piano; the choir, however, it appears, did not prove equal to the occasion. It was during this stay that Mendelssohn spent the pleasant hours with Queen Victoria and Prince Albert, of which he gives so graphic a description in his letters to his mother.

BERLIN, Oct. 8, 1842.

DEAR MRS. MOSCHELES, — I returned three days ago, and will not delay writing you a letter on this broad sheet of paper. What it will contain, you guess; but I write it in fear and trembling, for my mother assures me she has it from you yourself that you intended leaving Hamburg at the beginning of October, to return to England, without stopping at either Leipzig or Berlin. That would really be too bad! But I cannot quite believe it, and so venture to write you a regular letter of invitation: —

Mr. Felix Mendelssohn Bartholdy presents his compliments to Mr. and Mrs. Moscheles, and is simply craving for Mr. and Mrs. Moscheles's visit to Berlin for at least a fortnight. The country, music, and that sort of thing, in and about Berlin, are, to be sure, not worthy to be placed before them; if, however, a most hearty welcome can make the sandy soil appear fruitful, and the musicians inspired, nothing shall be neglected to produce the desired effect. The whole population of No. 3 Leipzigerstrasse joins in this most humble invitation. *Dinner on the table at three o'clock. Il y aura un violon.*

I wish you would say "Yes," and come. Would n't we enjoy it!

But, joking apart, dear Mrs. Moscheles, and you, my dear friend, should you still be in Hamburg, and these lines reach you there, then do not break our hearts by passing us by. Had I but known a little sooner when I should be here again, I should have written ere this; but we returned only four days ago from Switzerland and the South of Germany. Everything was uncertain, as it is still. However, here we are, and shall certainly remain for the next fortnight, so I say again, Come! If I could only send you a starling trained to say, Come! Come! True, my dear Moscheles, I should have nothing newer to show you in the way of compositions than the Song without Words in A major, which you had to hear but too often last spring. What with eating, drinking, walking, sketching, enjoying myself, and not caring for the morrow, I have not been able to write anything new. You, I am sure, will have all the more new and interesting things to show me. But even supposing we made no music at all, how delightful would it be to spend

26. MENDELSSOHN.

A BUST MODELLED FROM LIFE BY PROFESSOR RIETSCHEL

some time together in Germany! We should see and hear much more of one another, in peace and quietness, than we could in the rush of a London season, crowded as you are there with work, and I with leisure. You would meet Klingemann too; we are daily expecting him; he must have been in Hanover for some time already. Once more, to wind up, Come!

Now that our wanderings are concluded, we doubly feel what a happy summer we have spent, what English comfort we have enjoyed, what happiness and what never-to-be-forgotten kindness we have experienced. It was delightful indeed! And then, on our return home, we could not help saying that in the whole five months in which we wandered over land and sea, by steam or on muleback, across roads and rocks, we could not remember one unpleasant moment, not one dull day, but that we had been enabled to enjoy everything in undisturbed delight and health. Then I felt as though we never could be thankful enough, and ought never to pray for anything but a continuance of such happiness. From first to last we have felt deeply grateful for the mercies showered upon us, the remembrance of which will never leave us as long as we live. In Switzerland—oh, well, of that I could talk for whole evenings, till you were thoroughly tired of my long stories, as dull and dry as the incidents they would describe were lively and bright. Then came a delightful fortnight with the Souchays at

Frankfurt, then Leipzig and the first Subscription Concert. They flattered themselves you would have come to it, dear Moscheles; for David told me they had specially invited you. Hauptmann's first Mass was performed at St. Thomas's Church; then we had three new violin Quartets by Schumann, the first of which most particularly delighted me. Madame Schumann played Weber's Concertstück, and some Thalberg, as beautifully and with as much fire as ever. Here I found all well, — that is, music excepted, which, Heaven knows, is anything but well. They are performing "William Tell" for the wedding festivities, curtailed into three acts, and they call it "the composer's arrangement for the Parisian stage," and are racking their brains to discover whether Rossini had any call to write operas or not. The *Weissbier*, the cabs, cakes, and officials are wonderful here, but not much besides.

I have requested an audience of the King, with a view to obtaining his most gracious permission to depart; but what with the wedding, his journey, etc., I have not yet been received. Should I be more successful next week, I hope to be in my well-known Leipzig home in another fortnight; but it must be with a really good grace that he allows me to retire, for I love him too well, and owe him too much, to let it be otherwise.

Oh, how my pen has run away with me! I dare not touch the next page, which Cécile wants. So let me add, on this one, love to the children, and my wishes for your welfare, but, above all, the wish for an early and happy meeting.

Ever your

FELIX MENDELSSOHN BARTHOLDY.

LEIPZIG, Nov. 18, 1842.

MY DEAREST FRIEND, — How busy I have been lately you may gather from the fact of my only answering your delightful letter of the 20th to-day. But my chief reason for delay was that I wished to answer with due care and full consideration that part of it which mentions your intention of returning to Germany. This is a matter of so much importance to all of us, and I am so immensely delighted at the prospect, that at first I could not bring myself to think of it quietly and impartially. Now I have looked at it in every light, and of nothing else will I write to-day. If you really mean to leave England, — and from what you say I can no longer doubt you are in earnest, — this is the best time you could select, particularly if you thought of giving Berlin the preference. It appears to me that just now, when the King is so unmistakably anxious to secure for his capital artists of great reputation, a mere hint from you would suffice to elicit the most acceptable offers from that quarter. Such a hint is necessary, as, without it, nobody would believe, any more than I did at first, that you are really inclined to give up your position in England. Now, you have the very man in London to whom you might casually drop a word. You are on a confidential footing with him; and whilst, on the one hand, he has the warmest friendship and esteem for you, on the other, his suggestions and counsels have the greatest weight with the King of Prussia. Of course, I mean Bunsen.[1] If you were to speak to him, mentioning in a general way your intention of returning to Germany, I am sure a few words would suffice, and he would do his very best to secure to the King and to Berlin the honor of possessing you,—for as an honor any town of Germany you may select will look upon it. That, perhaps, you do not know; but then I do, most positively. To be sure, there is no official position — I mean no regular programme of musical duties — suitable for you, any more than there is for me, or for any musician whose heart is in his work; so my departure from Berlin would leave no place vacant for another to occupy. The very fact that no such place exists is the cause of my hesitating so long.

Now, however, it is decided that I am to have nothing to do with the Berlin public, but only with the King, whose qualities of head and heart I value so highly that they weigh heavier in the scale than half a dozen Berlin publics. Whether I am there or not, an excellent and honorable position would be open to you. But just think how delightful it would be if I did re-

[1] Bunsen was then the Prussian Ambassador accredited to the Court of Saint James.

turn, and we lived in the same place and saw our old dreams, that seemed so unattainable, actually realized! But that is a picture I will not attempt to draw in this letter. That I may have to return to Berlin, you see from the above. Probably it may be next year.

But suppose, now, that the thing you thought feasible in Berlin should take shape in Leipzig! Not that I should think of offering you the post I have held here, merely as conductor of the Subscription Concerts; but there is every reason to believe that that office may be supplemented by the directorship of a musical school, which will probably be started within the next twelvemonth. Might not a combination of that kind suit you? The salary would scarcely be more than twelve hundred thalers, to begin with; but I have no doubt things would soon improve all round. The King of Saxony will probably grant the funds requisite for founding the institution; and considering the influential and central position of Leipzig, I am confident that excellent results might be anticipated. The principal outlines of the scheme are to be settled before the end of the year. I am bound up with it, heart and soul. But then the first and most important question arises, Who is to be at the head of it? Now, just see how all difficulties would be at once solved if, in answer to that question, we could put your name! Regular lessons there would be scarcely any to give,—only the general supervision of the whole institution to undertake. You would have Hauptmann (who is at the head of the St. Thomas choir), David, Becker, etc., to work with you; and there would be the twenty Subscription Concerts to conduct.

Now, what do you think of it? Just turn it over in your mind, and let me know the result soon, very soon. I fancy these will not be the only letters we shall exchange on the subject. The matter is of importance, not only to yourself but to all Germany; and the former consideration, you know, would be quite enough for me.

So now give me your views as candidly as I have given you mine; and let me thank you a thousand times, and tell you how proud I am of being taken into your confidence. I do hope and trust we Germans shall get you back amongst us.

If you do not like to mention the matter to Bunsen, I am quite ready to look about for another opening. But Bunsen is the right man, I am certain. However, first of all, let us see what you think of the two different plans.

Kindest remembrances to your wife. I will try to fit an orchestral dress on to the Broadley piece; and if I succeed, will send it to you without delay. For the present, I am still without books or music, and have composed nothing but a Sonata for piano and cello. However, the boxes arrived yesterday; to-morrow we unpack them, and then we will set to work in good earnest.

Remain ever my friend, as I am yours,

Felix Mendelssohn Bartholdy.

The above-mentioned scheme concerning the establishment of a Conservatorio in Leipzig was carried out in March of the following year. The other plan, that of living and working together in the same city, was ardently pursued by the two friends, until it was realized in the autumn of 1846, when Moscheles left London to accept an appointment as professor at the Conservatorio of Leipzig. The next letters show the friendly spirit in which Mendelssohn worked to bring about the result, and the solicitude with which he entered into every detail that might smooth the path for Moscheles and make his new home attractive. Moscheles, on the other hand, did not hesitate to abandon the brilliant and more lucrative position he occupied in London, in order to devote himself, by the side of his friend, to what he believed to be the highest and truest aims of Art.

LEIPZIG, Jan. 16, 1843.

MY DEAR FRIEND, — I have to thank you and your wife for three very kind letters; excuse my not having done so before. At a time like that which we have passed through, when one feels completely unhinged and cannot regain one's peace of mind, when all seems dark and hopeless, it is but gradually one can attempt to return to one's occupations, even to the pleasantest of them.[1]

[1] He had lost his mother on the 12th of December of the preceding year.

During the first days of darkness not even music, or the thought of music, could afford me any consolation; but my old love for it soon returned, and now my little study, with its view on to the fields and far beyond, is a refuge, in which I gather fresh strength, and can sometimes feel more cheerful. Any attempt to divert my thoughts into another channel only tends to increase my sorrow, and leaves me more depressed than before. I am sure you will forgive my not having written sooner; you may read between the lines that I really could not have done so, and that even now I find it difficult to take up the pen.

The Scena for Mr. Broadley accompanies this letter. I have thrown in a Fugue, and fancy it is the best piece of the whole. It is the gingerbread-nut they give into the bargain at the sweet-stuff shop. The idea of it occurred to me in happier days, and I then scored the first three pieces; the fourth I had commenced when the great trouble came upon us, and I had to leave everything for weeks just where it was. Now I have finished it, and beg you to give it with my regards to Mr. Broadley. Perhaps I may write and enclose a line to him, besides. Thanks for your kind offer about publishers in England. Under other circumstances I would have accepted, as I have so often done before; but just now I need not trouble you, having every reason to be satisfied with my present publishers.

The transaction with Addison and Benedict was

of quite a different nature. Benedict told me last spring they wished to have my Symphony; that was all that was said about it. So I wrote to them offering it on the same terms as the former one. They certainly had given me a better price than the other publishers, either at that time or since. They thought it too much, and so I gave the piece to my ordinary publishers at the ordinary price, and therewith the matter ended. Lately, Benedict wrote me one of the kindest letters imaginable, that truly delighted and touched me, and in which I only regretted one thing, — that towards the end he mentions this long-forgotten incident. But the beginning is so kind and good that it would take a hundred such allusions to business transactions to outweigh the impression of his affectionate words. Tell him that, with my best love. And now I have not yet thanked you for your very kind and valuable present to Carl.[1] I was going to say you had given me more pleasure than him, because I so thoroughly enjoy these bright and graceful combinations; but the boy is so much in love with the music, and is so proud of his present from Uncle Moscheles, that nothing can surpass his delight, — in fact, you have started him on his musical career, for every morning after breakfast he insists on my

[1] The work alluded to, "The Harmonized Scales," Op. 97, is a series of fifty-nine pieces for a juvenile performer and his teacher; the former playing the scales in various time and rhythm, the teacher supporting him by a full accompaniment.

teaching him his notes. And the other day, when he had to write to his godfather Bendemann, and Cécile asked what she was to put for him to copy, he said, "I have got notes from Uncle Moscheles;" which he wrote somewhat in this style: —

ICH HABE

But, for all the crookedness of his letters, he feels just as happy and grateful as you or I would. Why, *our* letters are quite as crippled, if we compare them and their words to the sense they should convey.

I postpone saying anything in reference to the chief subject of our last letters till I am in a fresher and brighter mood. But I should like to know soon if you have really spoken to Bunsen, and what he said. The King of Prussia, I know, does not confine himself to native talent. Proposals would certainly not be expected *from* you, but would be made *to* you, whether coming from here or elsewhere.

Ever yours,

FELIX MENDELSSOHN BARTHOLDY.

LEIPZIG, April 15, 1843.

MY DEAR FRIEND, — Thanks for your letter of March 10, which was anything but a dry business memorandum, as it announced itself, but one of those kind and friendly letters which I always most heartily welcome. But now, do tell me what can have given you the idea that I was appointed Director of the Leipzig Music School, and that "all plans of our living together in Germany would vanish into thin air," etc. I am not appointed, and I am as anxious to have you here as ever, and confidently trust our plans will not prove castles in the air. You must have taken some newspaper paragraph for gospel truth; and you know that in my opinion they have been known to fall very short of that. These are really the facts:—

Three years ago I endeavored to found a music-school in Leipzig; and after endless interviews and exchanges of letters with some prominent men here, and also with the King, I felt, on my return from Berlin, that there was no time to be lost, and that it was a case of now or never. My engagements in Berlin did not allow of my accepting a permanent appointment here; but I took the matter in hand last November, and, having got the necessary funds, the school was opened, and I engaged to act as one of the teachers during the time I should remain here. I wrote to you then, and expressed my ardent desire to see you eventually at the head of the institution. Nothing has changed my desire since; only, what was then a long-cherished plan became four weeks ago a reality, and promises to bear good fruit.

Now, if we could only persuade you to come!

Whether I am here or not, it would be equally desirable to have you at the head of the institution. So far the Board of Directors is composed of only five gentlemen, none of whom are musicians. The six teachers are subordinate to them, but amongst themselves they are on an equal footing. But I believe that later on, when the institution develops, as seems very likely to be the case, a change will be necessary, and a musical man will have to join the Directors, or even to take the lead independently. And that is the position which, in connection with the Subscription Concerts, would be worthy of your acceptance. The difficulty is to get them to make you a definite proposal, both from a business and a musical point of view. No doubt, they would all like to have you here; but liking and wishing and thinking alone will not do it; and how absolutely necessary it is to come to a clear understanding in such matters, I should have learnt during the course of my negotiations in Berlin, had I not already been aware of the fact.

Have you received an offer from Prague to take the directorship of the Conservatorium there? Spohr's name was mentioned in connection with it, and so was yours. That he was asked, and that he refused, I know for a fact. I am anxious to hear whether there is any foundation for the rumor connecting your name with it.

I do not know what the appointment is like, but am enough of a patriot to wish that you lived in Germany rather than in England. The paper is at an end, so good-by.

Yours ever,

FELIX MENDELSSOHN BARTHOLDY.

LEIPZIG, April 30, 1843.

MY DEAR FRIEND,—Our last letters crossed on the road. A thousand thanks for yours that I received a few days ago. You know what heartfelt pleasure it gives me every time I see that well-known handwriting of yours on the address, and how grateful I am to you for writing to me, overwhelmed as you are by every kind of claim on your time. It would certainly be better if we need never correspond, and could exchange ideas verbally from one end of the year to the other, and that in Germany too! That is a prospect I am less than ever inclined to give up; only, I don't quite see my way to the where and the how. So, in the mean while, accept my thanks for the letter. The terms at our music school are two hundred thalers per annum; the cost of living here, at all decently, would amount at least to two hundred thalers. Young Englishmen, who usually live rather better, would probably require from two hundred and fifty to three hundred thalers,—say fifty or sixty pounds per annum.

The school has made a fair start; new pupils are almost daily joining, and the number of lessons and of teachers has had to be considerably increased. There are already thirty odd pupils, twelve of whom are instructed free of charge, and some of them are very promising.

We are afflicted, however, with two veritable maladies, which I mean to fight with all my might as long as I have anything to do with the institution. First, the Directors want to enlarge and to expand, — build houses and hire rooms, — whilst I maintain that for the next ten years the two large rooms that we have, and in which instruction can be given simultaneously, are quite sufficient. And then the pupils all want to compose and to theorize, whilst I believe that the principal thing that can and ought to be taught is sound practical work, — sound playing and keeping time, sound knowledge of sound music, etc. Out of that, all other knowledge grows of itself; and what is beyond is not a matter of teaching, but must come as a gift from above. Don't you agree with me? That I am not the man to turn art into mere mechanism, I need not say. But whither am I wandering? I have got into chatting instead of writing the two lines I intended. So now good-by.

Yours ever,

FELIX MENDELSSOHN BARTHOLDY.

In a letter of the 5th of April, 1844, Moscheles communicates to Mendelssohn the desire of the Handel Society, that Mendelssohn should prepare a new edition of the "Messiah." Moscheles had announced a concert for the 1st of June; and, in view of Mendelssohn's expected visit to England, he writes to ask him whether he is inclined to play on that occasion some new piece of his own composition for two performers. "Have you got anything of that kind amongst your manuscripts," he says; "or, if not, might not Jupiter evolve something Minerva-like from his fertile brain?"

LEIPZIG, April 12, 1844.

MY DEAREST FRIEND, — A thousand thanks for that dear, kind letter of yours, that I received (with the one from the Handel Society) just as I was leaving Berlin. Several weeks must elapse before I can knock at your door, as I shall be travelling slowly, and stopping at various places. But I will not postpone thanking you for your letter, and telling you how much pleasure it has given me. If you knew how deeply rooted is my heart-felt regard, how warm my admiration for you and your music, there would be no need to say how delighted I am that you will allow me to play at your concert and to appear in public by your side. But I know you are too unassuming ever to listen to anything of the kind; and the fact is, when it is put into words it really does not look genuine. So I had better write nothing more about it, — only this much, that I am at all times truly happy to make music with you, whether in public or in private. In whatever way you can use me, I am at your service. Let me write out parts, or collect tickets, or do anything else. If you can turn me to account, you will make me truly happy and grateful.

I do not think I have anything ready for two pianofortes. There are those Variations on a theme in B flat; I like them very well in a room, but they are not at all suited for public performance. What I should like best would be to write something new by that time; but time is short. Could not we play something on the organ, or even improvise together, or write ourselves a four-hand Fugue for the organ? Well, as I said before, you decide as to the what and how, and I am ready. At the latest, I shall be in London by the first week in May.

I have the greatest desire to accept the very gratifying offer of the Handel Society; but I have written to Macfarren to say that I cannot give a definite answer until I have had an opportunity of verbal communication. There can be no objection, I suppose, to the delay. Some of the editorial duties (especially preparing the Introduction) I doubt if I should be able to undertake; and that makes a verbal understanding desirable.

Thank you for correcting the proofs of my "Book of Songs;" thank you for the invitation to play at your concert; in fact, thank you for all these twenty years that I have known you, and in which you have shown me nothing but kindness.

Ever yours,

FELIX M.

27. Mendelssohn's Congratulations to

eles, May 30, 1844. (See page 245.)

Mendelssohn had been requested by the Handel Society to prepare an edition of the Oratorio "Israel in Egypt." Later on, a difficulty arose in reference to the notation. Moscheles says, in a letter to Mendelssohn: "A meeting was convened to discuss the subject; and after a lively debate it was decided that the only way to put before the public that notation which you saw in the original manuscript, and which you wish to adopt, would be to publish a fac-simile of it. But that, to be sure, would be out of keeping with the three works already published by the Society."

On the 8th of May Mendelssohn came to London, where he was as enthusiastically received as ever, whether he appeared before the public as a composer, a conductor, or a pianist. In Moscheles's concert he played, with him and Thalberg, Bach's Triple Concerto; in which his performance, and especially his improvisation of the Cadenza, is described as simply miraculous. On another occasion he played Moscheles's "Hommage à Handel," for two performers, with the composer; at the Philharmonic he conducted for the first time his "Walpurgisnacht."

As on former occasions, he was a constant and welcome guest in Chester Place. In celebration of Moscheles's birthday, he drew a second page of illustrations, referring to Moscheles's works, as a sequel to the one he made in 1832. "The writing," he says, "is again Emily's; the poem, Klingemann's; the design is again invented and the ink-blots omitted by Felix Mendelssohn Bartholdy." Amongst the various humorous allusions to Moscheles's works, we find his song "Silent Love," represented by a padlock closing the composer's mouth. The "March of intellect, Miss-understanding," allude to the "Harmonized Scales" written by Moscheles for his youngest daughter, Clara. The "Scène champêtre" illustrates the "Concerto Pastorale." "Les Roses et les épines de la dédication" show us Moscheles presenting his Concerto to Mendelssohn, who is bowing and profusely thanking, quite unconscious of the difficult passage which is lying in wait for him behind his back. The following is the translation of the lines in the centre of the page: —

> "On and still on, the journey went,
> Yet has he kept us all in view —
> Working in age with youth's content,
> In living — fresh, in loving — true." [1]

Mendelssohn left London on the 10th of July; two months later he and Moscheles met in Frankfurt. Another drawing illustrates an amusing incident at a concert that Moscheles gave in that city. It is described in a letter from Moscheles's daughter Emily: — [2]

"The room, long before the concert began, was crammed full, and still the people were coming. 'What will the Frankfurters say when they find no seats?' said Mendelssohn to Rosenhain. 'Let

[1] For the translation of these lines I am again indebted to Robert Browning. — EDITOR.

[2] See Illustration, No. 28.

us try to hire some chairs. Come along!' Off they were, but it was no easy matter to get chairs; for, it being the time of the fair, there were none to spare in the crowded hotels. At last they found four dozen in a small inn. 'These must be sent immediately,' says Mendelssohn. 'But who is to pay?' inquires the landlord. 'A great artist, Moscheles, who is giving a concert. It is all right; your money is safe.' 'Stop a minute!' says the canny landlord; 'those great artists often give concerts, pocket the money, and then disappear. I must have something down.' Mendelssohn and Rosenhain empty their pockets, which happen to be poorly filled. The landlord, however, is satisfied, and they hurry off to the concert-room with an instalment of chairs inside and outside their cab, the rest following.

"Another little incident that pleased Mendelssohn mightily, was a certain C far down in the bass, which my father unexpectedly put in as he was playing his A flat Study. 'That took me by surprise,' he said; 'it has a splendid effect, and ought not to be forgotten. I must put it down at once in Mrs. Moscheles's album.' He did so, drawing at the same time the cab, Rosenhain, himself, chairs, and all, but only half a horse. 'I can't draw that by heart,' he said."

FRANKFURT, March 7, 1845.

MY DEAR FRIEND, — It really was too kind of you to sit down and have a talk with me on paper, in the good old style. Now I will just leave everything to take care of itself till I have returned your chat and thanked you for your never-varying kindness to me. What you say of musicians and their doings in England, is certainly far from satisfactory; but where are doings ever satisfactory? Our inner life it is that is worth living; but then that is a very different thing to our outer doings, — something very much better. Conducting and getting up public performances is all very well in its way; but the result, even for the public, does not go far. A little better, a little worse, what does it matter? How soon it is forgotten! And what is it but our inner life, our calm and peaceful moments, that act and react on all this, that impel us and lead us onwards, taking all that public business in tow, and dragging it here and there, whichever way it should go?

That is the language of a Philistine (you will say), of a domestic animal, or a snail. And yet there is some truth in it; and one book of your "Studies" has had more influence on the public and on art than I don't know how many morning and evening concerts in I don't know how many years.

Do you see what I am driving at? I should so much like to get that four-hand Sonata of yours, or some four-hand Studies, or, for that, some two-hand ones, or whatever else you might send. But, to be sure, your season is beginning; and how little time is left you for composing and for your own

28. Incidents of a Concert at Frankfurt. A Pen Drawing by Mendelssohn. (See page 246.)

self, I know full well. But don't let the English Misses make you forget the German Misses, and their necessary adjuncts the Misters, who are waiting for that four-hand Sonata.

As for your feeling hurt by anything the Directors of the Philharmonic may have decided upon amongst themselves, I can only say you do them too much honor; their counsels can scarcely pretend to such distinction. On the contrary, I must confess that after I saw more of them last year, my good opinion was very much shaken, and my belief, too, in the future prospects of the Society. I very much doubt whether anything important can be expected of it; although, to be sure, the end will not come as long as the public opens its purse-strings. But the fact of the matter is, there are some very indifferent representatives of the musical profession that want to take the lead, and are allowed to do so; and the consequence is, as usual, that misunderstandings arise, intrigues follow, and the main object to be pursued is neglected. *C'est tout comme chez nous.* Do not ask where the *nous* is. It is everywhere. Just the old thing, — the inner life I was speaking of on the other page: *da capo del segno fino al* 𝄋 *e poi.*

I regret the difficulty with the Handel Society, but I cannot alter my views on the subject. On less important points I am ready to give way; as, for instance, in reference to the accidentals, — although there, too, I prefer the old method, on account of the long bars. But I cannot possibly introduce my marks of expression into a score of Handel's, nor my tempi, nor anything else, unless it is to be made perfectly clear what is mine and what Handel's; and as he has put his pianos and fortes and his figured basses where he thought them necessary, I must either omit them or leave the public in doubt as to which is his marking and which mine. It would be no great trouble to any one who agrees with my marking, to have it copied from the pianoforte arrangement into the score. On the other hand, it would be no slight evil if the edition did not clearly distinguish between Handel's and the editor's views. I must say that the interest I take in the Society is entirely dependent on the decision in reference to this point. The edition of the "Anthems" was so unsatisfactory, on account of the new marking, that I would never use it for the purposes of a public performance. I wish to know, above all things, what is Handel's and what is not. This desire the Council shared with me last year; but now the opposite views seem to prevail, and if they are adopted, I for one (and a good many with me, I believe) will much prefer the old edition, with its incorrect notes, to the new one with its various conceptions and consequent marking. All that I have written to Macfarren. I trust you are not angry with me for speaking out so plainly. My opinion is so intimately connected with what I have held to be right, all my life, that I could not possibly alter it.

We have had little music here lately. But one great treat was the performance, at a private house, of Cherubini's second Requiem, in D minor. They had given it six months' study, and it went accordingly. André has just sent the original score of Mozart's C major Symphony ("Jupiter") for my perusal. I must write out something from it for you that will amuse you. Eleven bars before the end, it formerly stood thus:—

The whole repetition of the theme he has written on an inserted leaf; the above passage is struck out, and only comes in three bars before the end. Is n't it a happy alteration? The repetition of the seven bars is one of the passages in that Symphony I love best.

But here our gossip must end.

Yours ever,

FELIX MENDELSSOHN BARTHOLDY.

"Israel in Egypt" was eventually edited by Mendelssohn, appearing in 1845–1846. On the titlepage and in the preface he most carefully guards against any possible misconception, and says: "The editor is alone responsible for the directions of 'piano' and 'forte,' and other marks of expression; for all such descriptions of the movements as stand within brackets (those which are not so placed being the only indications for which the original manuscripts furnish authority); for the suggestion of the tempi according to Maelzel's metronome; and for the figuring of the organ part. The adaptation of the instrumental parts for the pianoforte, intended as an accompaniment to the voices in the absence of the orchestra, is by the editor; for this, also, he alone is responsible."

FRANKFURT, April 12, 1845.

MY DEAR FRIEND, — You must have been as delighted at the news of Klingemann's engagement and the prospect of his being married soon, as I was. No, not quite so much; for when the news came, I danced about the room for fully five minutes, to the astonishment of Cécile, who thought I was out of my senses. Well, it has been a pet wish of mine for ever so long, and now that it is about to be realized I can scarcely believe it. I had given up all hopes of its coming to pass, and now that it has come I am doubly glad. It seems, too, so desirable and excellent a match that I feel sure it must bring happiness.

With us, thank Heaven, all is well. Cécile is in good health and spirits, the children are flourishing, spring is approaching; what more can mortal man desire?

You complain of the musical shortcomings in your part of the world. Well, things are not brilliant here; yet, for all that, one does occasionally get to hear something good. Add to that the balmy air of spring, the piano, and some sheets of music paper, and, after all, life is bearable.

Your old and very affectionate friend,

FELIX M. B.

BERLIN, Nov. 13, 1845.

MY DEAR FRIEND,—There is a rumor afloat in Leipzig, and I have met with it more than once since my return, that you might possibly take up your abode there, and devote yourself chiefly to the Conservatorio, thus carrying out, to the advantage of the Leipzigers, your old plan of settling in Germany. I must say I did not put much faith in the report. The difference between London and Leipzig is so great that I could scarcely fancy you would ever make up your mind to leave the former for the latter. But the other day I heard it asserted positively at an evening party that you had said you were disposed to settle in Leipzig. Some one had the news from Hamburg. Unlikely as it seems, I cannot help writing to ask whether there possibly might be some foundation for the rumor, and, secondly, whether I could do anything to convert such possibility into a certainty. I need not tell you how anxious I am to know, and how important the matter is, not only to me, but to all true lovers of music in Germany. So pray write as soon as possible how it really stands, and tell me point blank what steps should be taken to persuade you, if you are to be persuaded at all; or if you are only thinking of it in a general way and as a possible contingency, then just give me an outline of your ideas in an equally general way.

Nothing would be better and simpler, to be sure, if you really were inclined to decide for Leipzig, than to go straight there and to settle all details personally. But for the present, my only question is whether there is any truth at all in the report, or whether it is all idle talk, such as often gets about, without any foundation whatever. I believe, if you wrote to say there was a remote chance, the Leipzig Town Council would petition you in a body, the burgomaster at their head. Of my personal joy I say nothing to-day. I merely write as a Leipziger. When I heard the report the other day, I was suddenly seized with patriotic feelings for Leipzig, and I said to myself, "If I could but do something to bring this about!"

Good-by. I have been here for the last three weeks, to conduct performances of my "Athalie," "Œdipus," and some other things.

Yours ever,

F. M.

Moscheles writes:

Nov. 28, 1845.

My dear Friend, — As in the times of the Greeks the household gods were enthroned in every house and were surrounded by love and reverence, so you too have a special shrine devoted to you in Chester Place, — in our hearts rather and in our daily thoughts of you and yours. . . . Now let me first thank you for the cordial and hearty words you write on the prospects of my settling in Germany. My wishes in that direction are ever present, — smouldering embers that your friendly intervention, your influence, and, above all, the sacred spark of your genius, may kindle into a bright flame. Your questions remind me of those you put to me as we were walking arm in arm along the wide streets of London; they were the same, and now as then I have the same answer to give: Yes — yes — yes! I have grown indifferent to the so-called attractions of the great world; the taste of the day does not suit me, and I do not care to make any concessions to it, whether in public or in private life. What I aspire to, is an appropriate sphere of musical activity, interesting surroundings, you by my side, and finally Germany.

The position of head teacher of the pianoforte at the Leipzig Conservatorio would be very acceptable to me; and I readily assume that you are the

Director of the whole establishment, and that I could work in the same spirit that, from your first appearance in Leipzig, you infused into the art life of that musical centre.

LEIPZIG, Dec. 20, 1845.

MY DEAR FRIEND, — I most gladly take up the pen to-day; for I believe and trust that this letter may be instrumental in bringing about the realization of a wish which we Leipzigers, and more especially I personally, have long had at heart, remote as seemed the possibility of its fulfilment.

Yesterday I learned that the Directors of the Conservatorio were about to write to you officially. Their offers, which will be in your hands in a few days, will at least prove to you how fully they appreciate the desirability of securing you and your services for Leipzig. I hear they have based their proposals on the suggestions you made in your letter to me, and which I submitted to them on my return. The salary they offer you is more than double that of any other professor; they agree to the leave of absence, and, in fact, accede to one and all of your wishes. When you come to consider that they are ready to draw to the fullest extent on the means at their disposal, and further, that it would be hard to find elsewhere so influential and independent a position, I trust you will be disposed to accept their proposals. I feel all the more confident of the result, knowing, as I do, your ideas on the state of things here as compared with that in England, and remembering how much in earnest you were when we last talked the subject over.

The sum which is to be offered to you (if my information is correct) is small, according to English notions, but not so, measured by a German standard. Nor is it small when you take into consideration that it represents a fixed salary for only two or three lessons daily, and when you make allowance for the time of ten weeks' leave of absence; so that, if you choose to give two or three private lessons besides, you will be in a more remunerative position than most musical men in this country, and yet not have to give more than four or five lessons daily. That would be light work for you, accustomed as you are to the incredible exertions of London life. You would have leisure enough, and to spare; and what splendid fruit that might bear for art and for your friends! I cannot for a moment doubt that, under the circumstances, you will appreciate the change; and I must say that, from what I hear of the petty doings over there, and from what I experienced myself eighteen months ago, I can fully understand that every year brings you fresh cause for dissatisfaction, and a growing desire to turn your back on it all. And, really, the position you are asked to occupy is not unworthy of your acceptance.

One point I must answer, to correct a misapprehension: I am not, and never shall be, the Director of the school. I stand in precisely the same kind of position that it is hoped you may occupy. The duties of my department are the reading of compositions, etc.; and as I was one of the founders of the school, and am acquainted with its weak points, I lend a hand here and there until we are more firmly established. I look upon it as an element of stability that we should have no musical director placed in authority above the professors, — head masters, as we call them. These — Hauptmann, Becker, David, and myself (may I soon be able to add your name!) — form a committee of management on all musical matters, subordinate to the Directors only, inasmuch as these select the teachers, manage the business, and are generally the representatives of the Institute. But all musical matters are submitted to the committee of teachers, or to the special professor whom they may concern. So, for instance, any question relating to harmony would be referred to Hauptmann, whilst Becker would deal with what concerns the organ. The Board of Directors consists exclusively of prominent citizens, — non-musicians, — who give their services gratuitously.

And now let me request that if there is anything you do not wish to mention officially, you will inform me, and give me an opportunity of contributing to the success of a negotiation which may prove more fruitful in its results than any we have hitherto undertaken in the interests of music.

"I scarcely venture to hope, so much do I wish it," says your wife; and I, with a better right, echo her words, — for if you both only wish it half as much as I do, I fancy I may venture to hope.

And now, best thanks for your letter from Paris, that crossed mine on the road; and my congratulations on your successes, and the dedication at St. Cloud. As regards the Sonata[1] itself, it is of no use putting the many questions about it which I am so anxious and impatient to have answered; but I will make sure that Kistner lets me have the manuscript without an hour's delay. And just fancy, now, how grand it will be when we get that kind of thing before all kings of the French! I do believe the Leipzigers will get too proud; and yet I should be happy for their sakes. You see I can write of nothing else to-day. Good-by; let me hear from you soon.

Ever yours, F. M.

The following letter is in answer to Moscheles's question in reference to the cost of living in Leipzig: —

LEIPZIG, Jan. 17, 1846.

MY DEAR FRIEND, — Your last letter, and that of your wife, gave me the greatest pleasure, for they seem to hold out a promise that our wish to

[1] The Sonate Symphonique for two performers (Op. 112), which Moscheles, with his daughter Emily, had played at the Court of King Louis Philippe, to whom the work was dedicated.

have you here will be fulfilled. I do hope and trust we are not mistaken. On the day that brings your consent I will drain my best bottle of wine, and cap it with a cup of champagne. I hasten to answer your questions, having duly consulted my wife and her account-books with the following result: The price of a flat — consisting of seven or eight rooms, with kitchen and appurtenances — varies from three hundred to three hundred and fifty thalers.[1] For that sum it should be handsome and cheerful; and as regards the situation, should leave nothing to be desired. Servants would cost about one hundred to one hundred and ten thalers per annum, all depending, to be sure, on what you require. Male servants are not much in demand here, their wages varying from three to twelve thalers per month. A good cook gets forty thalers a year; a housemaid, thirty-two. If you add to these a lady's-maid, who could sew and make dresses, you would reach about the above-mentioned figure. Should you require, in addition to these, a man-servant, that, to be sure, would increase the expense; but living as others do here, I think you would scarcely need one. Wood — that is, fuel for kitchen, stoves, etc. — is dear, and may amount to one hundred and fifty or two hundred thalers for a family of five, with servants. Rates and taxes are next to nothing: eight or ten thalers a year would cover all. In a word, I think you would live very well and comfortably on from

[1] The thaler equals three shillings, or seventy-five cents.

eighteen hundred to two thousand thalers. It is difficult to fix the terms for your lessons, even approximatively, for there is no precedent in Leipzig to go by. Madame Schumann-Wieck had two thalers, but at that price found only few pupils, and those mostly among foreigners spending a short time here. I think that would be different with you, and am confident that if you chose to say one thaler and a half you would be overrun by applicants. The same probably would be the case at two thalers. And so I return to what I said in my last letter: I believe that, putting together the salary from the Conservatorio and what you would make by private lessons and the publication of compositions (even if you published ever so little, but I trust it would be ever so much), your income would suffice for your expenditure, and it would still be open to you to draw on your capital or to leave it to bear interest. I do not think I have in any way looked at things in too favorable a light in giving you these estimates. I certainly made them after due consideration, and in accordance with my experience of this place.

Now I have but to add that I have no doubt your furniture will be allowed to pass free of duty (in fact, I don't mind making bold to guarantee that at once); further, that I certainly have composed a "Lauda Sion" for a church festival at Liege; and finally, that we are all well, and thinking of you, and expecting with the greatest impatience your next letter, which is to bring us the welcome news that you are coming.

Ever yours,

FELIX MENDELSSOHN BARTHOLDY.

Moscheles writes:—

LONDON, Jan. 26, 1846.

A thousand thanks, my dear friend, for that kindest of letters. In its way it is as complete as you are yourself in all your creations. Whether at the Piano or the Organ, from the Song to the Oratorio, in Canon, Fugue, or Symphony; with the pen (*vide* certain birthday illustrations) or with the brush on the Bridge of Sighs — always the same: bright, gifted, and genial. I am only sorry that my warm appreciation of your qualities gives me no great advantage over your other admirers; however, in one respect I am in advance of them, and that is, in the thanks I owe you. My answer to the Directors I enclose; please seal and deliver it.

On the 3d of February Moscheles writes:—

"Elated as we were at the prospect before us, our spirits were further raised by an unexpected invitation to conduct the Birmingham Festival that I received the other day. Coupled with that, is the good news that you have promised to take part in it, and to produce a new work of yours on that occasion; so you can fancy that all is indeed sunshine to me."

LEIPZIG, Feb. 11, 1846.

Hurrah! your decision is taken, you are coming! Let every one of these lines rejoice! A more welcome piece of news I have not received since I have been here, and one that promises so rich a harvest for all of us. There was a flutter of excitement, such as I have never witnessed in our ranks, when I produced your letter at the Board meeting the other day. I had kept it all to myself, to lay before the Directors on that occasion; and when the time came, I announced that I had received your answer, and here it was with your acceptance, black on white. They were for answering at once; but as there were several of them, it took a few days, so that you get their letter with mine to-day. Not only the leave of absence for three months, but anything and everything you may desire, will, I am sure, be agreed to. In fact, it is in everybody's interest that you should be made perfectly comfortable; and I do believe you will be satisfied, and will not be unfavorably impressed by the difference between the stirring metropolis and our petty provincialism. This much is certain, that you can nowhere find better intentions, and a heartier desire on all sides to make you feel at home, than here. Since the Fates have decreed that you shall return to Germany, and since you cannot, in this most excellent but somewhat peculiar country, hope to escape a certain amount of gossip and twaddle, whichever place of abode you may select, I think you will have no reason to regret your choice having fallen on Leipzig, and I trust you will like it better and better every year.

My personal feelings I cannot adequately express. How could I tell you what it is to me, when I think that you are really coming; that you are going to live here for good, you and yours, and that what seemed a castle in the air is about to become a tangible reality; that we shall be together, not merely to run through the dissipations of a season, but to enjoy an intimate and uninterrupted intercourse? I shall have a few houses painted rose-color as soon as you really are within our walls. But it needs not that; your arrival alone will give the whole place a new complexion. But what is the use of my scribbling, when you are coming, and we can thank you verbally? Not that that is necessary; you know too well, without words, how overjoyed we are. Cécile will write a few words for herself.

Now, you must soon let me have a long, domestic, non-musical letter, like my last one, so that we can arrange and settle various things for you before you arrive. Is n't it delightful that we have got to that point already?

Your second letter, with the Birmingham news, just comes too. They have truly done well in securing you as a conductor; and how splendid it would be if we could meet there! About my "Elijah," however, I shall not be able to decide

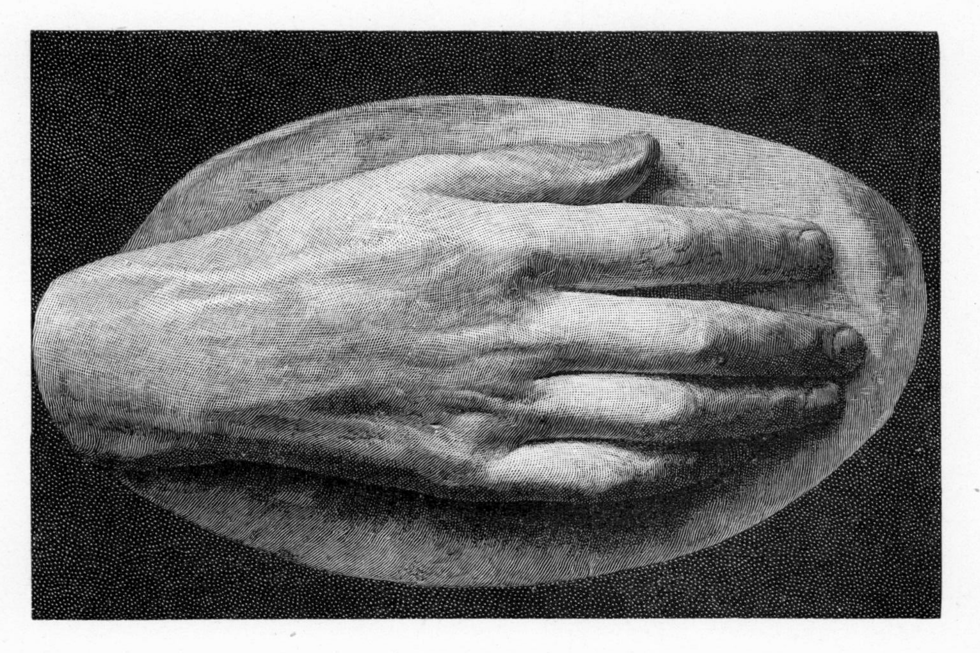

29. From a Cast of Mendelssohn's Hand.

anything before the middle of next month. The fact is, my health frequently leaves much to be desired; and all this conducting and performing often fatigues me greatly. At such times I scarcely believe I shall be strong enough to go through a musical festival again. If I possibly can, I most certainly shall go; but as there is considerable doubt of my being able to do so, I am doubly glad to know that the matter is in your hands, feeling sure that thus all must go well.

The letter to Jenny Lind I have sent to Berlin; and when I see her a few weeks hence, I will put it strongly to her, but I scarcely believe she will be at liberty to accept. It is wonderful how she is sought after on all sides, and I believe her engagements are fully made up to the end of the year.

Beethoven's "Ruins of Athens," or rather my selections from that work, would be appropriate, but they have not yet appeared in print. I believe Ewer & Co. have the score and the copyright. Pischek, I trust, you will be able to secure; he would be an important acquisition. More of all that next time. For to-day, good-by. Once more, thanks and — hurrah! you are coming!

Ever yours,

Felix.

In reference to the "Sonate Symphonique," Mendelssohn wrote to Messrs. Stern & Co., publishers, in Berlin: —

LEIPZIG, March 20, 1846.

TO MESSRS. STERN & CO., *Music Publishers, Berlin:*

GENTLEMEN, — Kapellmeister Taubert, who is leaving to-morrow for Berlin, brings you the proofs of Moscheles's Sonata. I have played it with him, and have looked it carefully through without having discovered a single fault, and am happy to find the work of my friend and teacher so judiciously and correctly presented. I am

Yours truly,

FELIX MENDELSSOHN BARTHOLDY.

LEIPZIG, April 20, 1846.

MY DEAR FRIEND, — Many thanks for your last letter, which I received yesterday. Although I dare say you have heard through Klingemann that I hope to complete my Oratorio, I write myself to-day to tell you so. If my health continues as satisfactory as it is at present, I feel confident I can be ready in time, and will give some sheets to the copyist within the next few days, with a view of forwarding them to you without delay. Towards Whitsuntide I trust the chief pieces of the first part and some of the second will be in your hands. That will be soon enough, will it not? I am still undecided whether I shall have the parts printed, as Mr. Moore desires. Why should they not be copied out just as well? If, contrary to expectation, I should not have finished, I have enough other manuscripts in readiness, so that I might, as Mr. Moore suggests, conduct some other new piece of mine. My "Athalie," for instance, is now in England, and, if I am not mistaken, is being translated by Bartholomew; so, if the worst comes to the worst, those Choruses could be sung. But, as I said before, I trust that will not be necessary; and if it is not otherwise decreed, I most surely mean to go to Birmingham. How delightful to see you all again! Excuse my writing so hurriedly; I am quite incapable of putting together a sensible letter. — But just one more question: Is it not quite time that you should give me your orders for Leipzig? That you will be here by next autumn, I take for granted, and my wife and I ought to set about making all the necessary preparations. So please let us know.

Thanks for your kind and friendly words in reference to my work, and a thousand thanks for that beautiful four-hand Sonata of yours, the proofs of which I corrected and then got as a present into the bargain. I only wish the time had come already for us to sit together at the piano and play it.

Best love to your wife and children from

Yours ever,

FELIX.

LEIPZIG, May 8, 1846.

MY DEAR FRIEND, — In about a fortnight I hope to send you the score of the first part of my Oratorio (with the exception of some of the Solo numbers), that is to say, considerably more than one half of it. The Choruses of the second part will, I trust, be in your hands in June, the rest to follow early in July. I should much like Bartholomew to make the translation, with Klingemann's occasional advice. Could that be managed? Then I absolutely require a first-rate high baritone. Can such a one be found? And what I most require now is an answer to my last letter, saying that you are all well and happy, and thinking of me.

Yours ever,

FELIX MENDELSSOHN BARTHOLDY.

LEIPZIG, May 11, 1846.

MY DEAR FRIEND, — I see by Mr. Moore's letter, which you enclosed, that he would rather have the parts printed. I have no objection; but the question arises whether an English firm would be ready to publish them under the conditions that Simrock agreed to; namely, that any alterations I might think necessary should be made in the plates, even if that necessitated new ones being engraved. Will you be so kind as to talk this point over with Mr. Buxton, of Ewer & Co., to whom I should best like to give the manuscript for publication. As there are so many copies required for Birmingham (42 Sopranos, 20 Violins, etc.), I have no doubt of his assent.

Then there is another point on which I want your help, or at least your advice. I mean the question of terms for the work (Choral edition, etc.). What do you think I ought to ask for it in England? I wished Mr. Buxton to make me an offer, as I had had some applications for the copyright from other quarters; and whilst giving him the preference, I should not like him to be the loser, or to lose myself by the transaction. He, however, leaves the matter entirely in my hands, and says he will be agreeable to whatever I propose. What do you think, in justice to him and to myself, I ought to ask? Please give me your advice; this matter ought to be settled before the parts are printed. But now please let me have definite instructions by return of post whether I am to send the score only, or a copy of the parts also. If, as Mr. Moore desires, I am to send the latter, that will not prevent my forwarding the score of the first part of the Oratorio to you in ten or twelve days; so that the translation can be made from that, whilst the parts can be copied from my manuscript.

If after all there is no baritone to be got, the whole thing falls to the ground and the Oratorio cannot be performed. Are neither Pischek, Staudigl, or Oberhöfer *possible*, as the French say? The latter, I believe, does not know English; so it rests with the two others. Good-by. Don't forget instructions about house-hunting in Leipzig. Please copy the enclosed; it too concerns the Birmingham Festival. Excuse trouble and haste.

As ever yours,

FELIX M. B.

P. S. How would it be if I had the orchestra parts printed in Germany and brought them over with me? The vocal parts, at any rate, would have to be printed in England, on account of the English words.

Of the singers named, it was Staudigl who was eventually selected to sing the part of Elijah at Birmingham.

In answer to Mendelssohn's question, what terms he should make for the copyright of his Oratorio, Moscheles writes: —

"I quite feel the responsibility of advising you in the matter; for if fifty years hence it is said, 'Mendelssohn received only so many pounds sterling for this grandest of works, this inexhaustible mine of wealth to the editor, and that at the suggestion of Moscheles,' my ashes will be disturbed in their rest. Well, well, you will nod your venerable head, and say, 'Never mind; Moscheles meant well.'

"You do not say what other offers you had, besides that from Buxton. I think you will find him straightforward in his dealings, and ready to recognize that the market value of your productions is constantly increasing. So I should say you might ask £50 more than you did for the 'Hymn of Praise.'

"One point to take into consideration is whether this work is richer than the other in Solos, these being a better source of income to the publisher than Choruses."

Moscheles had probably forgotten the fact that Mendelssohn received only £25 for his "Hymn of Praise" from Messrs. Novello. The same firm bought the copyright of his "Elijah," in June, 1847, for 250 guineas.

It may be interesting to mention here some of the prices given for other works of Mendelssohn by Messrs. Novello. For his music to Sophocles's "Antigone," £30 10*s.*; Duo for Piano and Violin in D, Op. 58, £12 12*s.*; "Walpurgisnacht," £24; Music to "A Midsummer Night's Dream" (not including Overture), £47 5*s.*; "Hear my Prayer, O Lord," £4; Concerto for Violin and Orchestra, Op. 64, £10 10*s.*; Book 6 of "Songs without Words," Op. 67, £25; Trio in D minor for Piano, Violin, and Violoncello, Op. 49, £10 10*s.*; Trio in C minor for ditto, Op. 66, £20; Six Songs, Op. 71, £20.

LEIPZIG, May 23, 1846.

MY DEAR FRIEND, — As I am leaving this evening for the Rhine, and have not yet heard from you in answer to my last letter, I send to-day a complete copy of the first part of my "Elijah" to Messrs. Hüttner & Co., Ewer's correspondents in Hamburg, to be forwarded to you through Mr. Buxton. I enclose also a copy of the words. This and the score please place at once in Mr. Bartholomew's hands, for the purposes of translation.

May you find something in my score to please you; and may you at least recognize my good intentions, and reward them with your usual kindness and friendship!

Ever yours,

FELIX.

The next letter refers to the following incident: Mendelssohn had conducted the Philharmonic Concerts during the season of the preceding year. On one occasion he arrived late at a rehearsal, owing to unavoidable causes, and was so discourteously received by some of the members of the orchestra that he laid down his baton and refused to proceed. Some of the Directors who were present succeeded, not without difficulty, in pacifying him; the offenders were requested to leave the room, and he was finally persuaded to resume his office.

LEIPZIG, June 26, 1846.

MY DEAR FRIEND, — The occasion of these lines is a passage in Mr. Moore's letter, in which he says: "Nearly the whole of the Philharmonic band are engaged; a few only are left out, who made themselves unpleasant when you were there."

Now, I strongly object to this restriction; and as I fancy you can exercise your authority in the matter, I address my protest to you, and beg you to communicate it to Mr. Moore. There is nothing I hate more than the reviving of bygone disputes; it is bad enough that they should have occurred. This one of the Philharmonic is, as far as I am concerned, dead and buried, and must on no account have any influence on the selection made for the Birmingham Festival. If men are to be rejected because they are incompetent, that is not my business and I have nothing to say in the matter; but if it is because "they made themselves unpleasant when I was there," I consider that an injustice, against which I protest. Any further disturbance on the part of these gentlemen, I am sure, is not to be feared. That at least is my belief, shared probably by all concerned. So you will sincerely oblige me by having the selection made exactly as if I were not coming to England. The only consideration that can be shown me is not to take me into consideration at all. You will do me a favor by putting this very strongly to Mr. Moore, and requesting him to let the matter drop. If my wishes are to be complied with, the incident must herewith end. Should it be otherwise, I shall write another dozen letters in protest against what I should consider a spirit of vindictiveness. Excuse all this. Ever yours,

FELIX.

LEIPZIG, July 12, 1846.

MY DEAR FRIEND, — In answer to your letter let me say without delay that the last time I passed through Birmingham the touch of the organ appeared to me so heavy that I could not venture to perform upon it in public. If however it is materially improved, I shall be happy to play one of my Sonatas; but I should not wish this to be announced before I had tried the organ myself.

With great pleasure, or rather with — Well, you know what it is to me to sit at the piano with you, and it needs no words to assure you that I am at all times ready. You decide, please, what it shall be; my head is quite full of "Elijah" just now. The Double Concerto of Bach is beautiful, but not brilliant; that of Mozart rather the other way. Anyhow, I will bring the former. But I must really be excused as regards playing a Solo. As it is, I feel the strain of conducting more than I used, and am no longer capable of playing a Solo and conducting a new piece of my own at the same concert. Some other instrumental number had better be put on the programme; that seems to me more appropriate, too, than having two pieces for the piano. Now, please let me know soon the date fixed for the Festival, as Mr. Moore has not yet informed me; also who is going to sing the Solos in my Oratorio. When "Saint Paul" was performed in Birmingham, it was followed by a selection from Handel's Oratorios; I much disapproved of this, and trust it is not to be the case this time.

Please answer all these questions, and tell me the latest date you can allow for my arrival;

30. Medallion of Mendelssohn. Modelled by Knauer, of Leipzig, soon after the composer's death, and presented to the Directors of the Gewandhaus.

earlier I shall not be able to come, but I hope I may find time to remain a little afterwards. In the course of next week I will send the last part of the manuscript.

It is not yet settled whether my wife goes with me, but I think she will.

With kindest messages, ever yours,

FELIX M. B.

LEIPZIG, July 28, 1846.

MY DEAR FRIEND, — Many thanks for your letter of the 18th, giving me the dates of the Festival and of the rehearsals. Your and Mr. Moore's former letters had not stated these definitely; but now that I know them I can make my plans accordingly, and will be in London on the 17th, in good time for the rehearsal of the 20th. I should be glad if the Solos could be rehearsed at the piano on the 19th.

As the morning performances are to last three hours, the "Elijah," which according to my calculation takes two hours, will not be enough by itself. But then I hope it can be so arranged that a whole piece, not a selection, can be given in addition to it, in the same way as the "Stabat Mater" stands on the programme for the first day. To be sure, it must rest with the Committee whether they will give one or two pieces before; but, however that may be, don't let us have a ragout afterwards. If there must be three hours, do pray arrange it so that a single piece of three quarters of an hour's duration be chosen. Besides, it would be a pity to spoil a programme which, as a whole, has a certain look of distinction about it.

And now I hope and trust we may soon meet again. Best love to all. My Cécile, I am sorry to say, will not be able to accompany me; too many reasons stand in the way of her doing so.

Yours ever,

FELIX MENDELSSOHN BARTHOLDY.

Notwithstanding Moscheles's efforts, Mendelssohn's wishes were not complied with. After the performance of the Oratorio, Mario sang an air from Mozart's "Davide penitente," Grisi an air by Cimarosa, and the concert ended with a Chorus by Handel.

LEIPZIG, Aug. 9, 1846.

MY DEAR FRIEND,—Once more a line (as our letters have crossed) to say that I hope to be in London on the 17th, travelling *viâ* Ostend and Dover.

All else about Miss Bassano, etc., verbally.

I have just gone through the orchestra parts of the Oratorio, and have corrected a number of faults, whereby I hope to have saved you much time. Good-by,—soon to meet.

Yours ever,

FELIX M. B.

On the 18th of August Mendelssohn arrived in London, and on the following day a first rehearsal of the Solos was held at Chester Place. The Oratorio was performed on the 28th of August. On the 29th Moscheles wrote: "Your visit to Birmingham, and the production of your 'Elijah,' have opened a new world of art to me; your work has made an impression on my mind that can never be effaced. If I did not tell you so last night, when so many were pressing forward to congratulate you, it was because I fancied I felt more, and had more to say, than they. Besides, I preferred writing, to tell you how deeply impressed I am; for if I do so verbally, you will only give me the obsolete answer that dates from your boyhood, — 'There is much room for improvement; give me your advice,' etc., — and that, from you to me, is out of place. Improve, correct, as much as you think right; tell me why and wherefore you make this or that alteration; let me learn from you, and gratefully acknowledge that it is so. You might well put Beethoven's motto,[1] 'Man, help thyself!' on your coat

[1] This has reference to an incident which occurred when Moscheles, then twenty years of age, was residing in Vienna. In 1824 Beethoven's "Fidelio" was produced, and Moscheles was commissioned to make the pianoforte arrangement of that work. In his diaries of those days we find various entries recording his visits to Beethoven. The alterations suggested by the master were made with due care and deference, and the completed arrangement was finally left at Beethoven's rooms. On the last page of the manuscript Moscheles had written, "End, with the help of God." When the manuscript was returned four characteristic words had been added, in Beethoven's bold and all but illegible handwriting: "Mensch, hilf dir selber!" (Man, help thyself!)

of arms; for God has endowed you with rare gifts, that permit you to approach Him in the true spirit of devotion and reverence."

HOBART PLACE, EATON SQUARE, Aug. 29, 1846.

MY DEAR FRIEND, — Your letter, which I just receive, makes me truly happy. Let me thank you cordially for the friendly sympathy and for the indulgence with which you have listened to my music. Your kind words of praise are more to me than words from any other quarter, and a great deal more than I deserve, according to my own estimation. Thanks, thanks! that is all I can say just now, although I should like to add so much. But I will wait till we meet in a day or two, or perhaps till we are taking some quiet stroll together round the city walls of Leipzig or elsewhere. Thanks again, and may you ever preserve your friendship and kind indulgence for me.

Yours for ever and a day,

FELIX MENDELSSOHN BARTHOLDY.

LEIPZIG, Oct. 8, 1846.

MY DEAR FRIEND, — I hasten to answer your kind steamer letter, and to say that I ordered the rooms in the "Blumenberg" a few days after my return, according to the memorandum in my pocket-book, which your wife dictated. I called once more at the hotel, on receiving your letter, and made sure that all was prepared for your arrival on the 21st. The maid with the requisite capacity for sewing is engaged, and we have been offered two most eligible suites of rooms for you, which are now anxiously awaiting your arrival.

The main point, however, I want to answer, my dear Moscheles, is that referring to your best mode of travelling. I must decidedly advise you to take *Extrapost*, not only because it is far more convenient when you are a party of five going so long a distance, but because I believe it to be no more expensive, in fact rather less so, than the *Schnellpost*, *Courier*, or any other means of conveyance, all necessitating your travelling day and night. The only difficulty might be your not having a carriage of your own, — that is, if, as I believe, you have not taken one with you. But it just happens that my mother-in-law, who is here, intends returning to Frankfurt towards the end of the month or early in November, and wishes to take *Extrapost*. Now, if you could hire a carriage, you would have the use of it one way, and my mother-in-law would be glad to take it for the return journey. Thus the only difficulty is overcome, and you would be obliging her into the bargain. I have not the slightest doubt this mode of travelling would be far the most convenient and agreeable for all of you, and therefore most decidedly advise it in preference to any other. You know that if you want to travel as quickly in Germany as you do in England, you must not take *Extrapost*, but *Courier*-horses, which is expensive, although not as compared to England. If however you do not care for such extra speed, you give the postilion a tip of ten or twelve groschen, and you will do the German mile in about three quarters of an hour. Leaving at seven o'clock in the morning, you will be the first evening in Butlar, the second in Weimar, where you will find very good accommodation in the Erbprinz. Please let me know when you start, and about what time you expect to be here, so that we may meet and welcome you on your arrival.

Everybody here is rejoicing at the prospect of your coming, especially the musicians, more especially those of the Conservatorio; but far ahead of any of them,

Yours,

FELIX M. B.

Moscheles writes that he expects to arrive on the 21st of October, and adds: "I go to Leipzig hopeful of the future, and filled with the most pleasant expectations. On the one hand I look back to England and its art-aspiring people with the warmest appreciation. On the other I rejoice at the prospect of living amongst the cultivated and art-loving citizens of Leipzig." He arrived on the day fixed, when, as his diary says, Mendelssohn received him with the affection of a brother, and rendered him the services of a practised courier. The long-cherished plan was realized, and

Moscheles soon entered on his new duties at the Conservatorio.

Moscheles was soon comfortably settled in his new quarters in Gerhard's Garten, — a spot of historical interest. There the Battle of Leipzig was once fiercely contested; now, however, it was peaceful and pleasant enough to make an exceptionally charming place of abode.

At the Conservatorio Moscheles entered on his new duties, which proved as congenial to his taste as he had expected. The pleasures, too, of daily musical and friendly intercourse with Mendelssohn he now enjoyed to the fullest extent.

On the 6th of January Moscheles writes: "It was a pleasant evening we spent at the Mendelssohns'. Our Felix was invited too, and was privileged to enjoy such music as usually falls to the lot of the initiated only. Joachim, our favorite, was there also. Mendelssohn played us some parts of his yet unpublished 'Elijah,' in which, since its performance in Birmingham, he has made sundry alterations, to which he attaches much importance; for instance, in those passages where the widow seeks help of Elijah he has given much more prominence to the part of the prophet."

January 24. — "With David at Mendelssohn's, who played and sang parts of his 'Elijah' to us. Among the changes and additions he has made, I was particularly struck by a Terzet in D major for two sopranos and one alto. All seems now to combine to make this work as varied as it is great."

January 28. — "Mozart's G minor Symphony at the Gewandhaus. Mendelssohn took the time of the last movement more moderately than is usually done, all chromatic modulations thus being brought out much more clearly than I have been accustomed to hear them."

During a choir rehearsal of the "Elijah" in the Gewandhaus, Moscheles took notes of some of Mendelssohn's directions: —

"'Out with the vowels! The h*ea*–thens. Who made the heavens and the w*a*–ters.'

"No. 5. 'Rather err on the side of vigor than on the side of drowsiness.'

"No. 8. 'From the very beginning the music must sound fresh — not only towards the end.'

"No. 20. 'I want to hear *Tone,* — what one might call *Music.*'"

Mendelssohn's last birthday, the 3d of February, 1847, was celebrated by his friends in Gerhard's Garten. Old and young had made festive preparations for the occasion; in the Moscheleses' drawing-room a stage had been erected, and every scrap of domestic talent was enlisted to entertain the hero of the day. Cécile Mendelssohn and her sister, Mrs. Schunck, opened the proceedings with a comic dialogue between two lady's-maids, spoken in the Frankfurt dialect. Then the word "Ge-wand-haus" was enacted as a charade. Joachim, adorned with an eccentric wig, appeared as Paganini, and executed a brilliant improvisation on the G-string (in German, *Ge*-Saite). The scene between Pyramus and Thisbe in the "Midsummer Night's Dream" followed and stood for *Wand* (wall). To illustrate the syllable *Haus* (house), Mrs. Moscheles had written a little domestic scene; and when, in the course of this, Moscheles, dressed as a cook, made his appearance, Mendelssohn burst into a truly Homeric fit of laughter. He was sitting in a large wicker-work arm-chair; and as, in the fulness of his enjoyment, he rocked to and fro, the chair joined in, bending and creaking in sympathetic rhythms. It was not till after a long interval that the cook could get a hearing. As a finale, the whole word was represented by the combined juvenile forces of the two families, each of the children being provided with some instrument, and Felix Moscheles wielding the conductor's baton. Joachim led with a toy-violin. Of however doubtful a nature this musical treat may have been to Mendelssohn, he certainly entered most fully into the spirit of the thing, and appreciated every allusion to the real Gewandhaus; especially when Joachim made certain remarks in imitation of the master himself, Mendelssohn started off again, and the endurance of the sympathetic arm-chair was put to the utmost test.

After the performance, actors and public adjourned to the first floor, occupied by the Schuncks. In the centre of the supper-table stood the birthday cake, around which burned thirty-seven candles. At the foot of each, Mrs. Moscheles had written a few words descriptive of the year it represented, — from the cradle to the piano and the conductor's desk; from his first attempt at composition to "Saint Paul," "Elijah," and the "Opera *in spe*." In the centre stood the "Light of Life," that was so soon to fail!

In the month of April of this year Mendelssohn visited England for the last time. He conducted three performances of "Elijah" in Exeter Hall, and was again active at the Philharmonic Concerts. On his return from England, the news reached him of the death of his sister Fanny Hensel. To her he had been linked throughout life by the closest musical sympathy and affinity, and it was thought he never quite recovered from the shock caused by her sudden death, rendered doubly painful by its occurring during his absence from Berlin, and at one of her own musical matinées.

At this time Moscheles and his wife, who were making a short visit in England, received the following letter from Mendelssohn: —

BADEN-BADEN, June 9, 1847.

MY DEAR MRS. MOSCHELES, — When I received your very kind letter, but could not answer it at once in the hurry of the last London days, I pictured to myself the pleasure of writing to you in a cheerful, pleasant tone, from some favorite spot in Switzerland, perhaps with illustrations or something of the sort. Now all that is changed. You know the heavy affliction which has befallen us, and how our inward and outward life has been shaken to its innermost depths, for a long, long time to come, perhaps forever. I am sure you sympathized with us in our irreparable loss, although you and Moscheles knew my sister but little. You can fancy, however, what I feel, — I, to whom she seemed present at all times, in every piece of music, and on all occasions, whether of happiness or of sorrow. Indeed, such is the case with us all; words are nothing at such a time; and yet I cannot speak of anything else. Forgive me, then, if these lines contain little else than hearty thanks for the letter above mentioned, which was another kindness added to the many which followed every step of my last visit to London.

We shall not go to Switzerland under the circumstances; for we could not now derive any real pleasure from the journey, and probably I shall return to the North sooner than I intended. I often feel irresistibly drawn to Berlin, where my youngest sister is now all alone. My brother has been here for the last week; and certainly nothing can do us so much good as our walks in the woods, the secluded and regular life we are leading here, and, above all, the hours we spend with the children. My brother has brought his contingent of young people; and they, as well as mine, are in excellent health and spirits, and delight everybody who sees them. Cécile too is quite well, thank Heaven; however, deeply afflicted.

I hope to hear a favorable account of your visit to England, and trust you will not remain too long; so that the Leipzigers, and, above all, those pianoforte pupils of yours, may get their full share of that instruction which they are thirsting for. The Londoners will, to be sure, say the same thing; but you have spent so many years amongst them that you must now do something for the German cockneys, or country cousins, or whatever you may choose to call them, whose faults I know as well as anybody, but who have also their good and admirable qualities, provided one can get over their cockneyism and old-fashioned ways. But that requires time, and it is for this reason I want you to come soon. What! I hear you say, that I may lose no time in getting used to the manners and customs of the natives? No, I answer; but to help us wage war on the pigtail.

Remember me kindly to all our dear English friends. I need not say that this letter is meant for Moscheles as well. Heaven grant health to you and yours! and remember kindly your

FELIX MENDELSSOHN BARTHOLDY.

Of the numerous notes exchanged after Mendelssohn's return we transcribe only the following:

LEIPZIG, Oct. 7, 1847.

MY DEAR FRIEND, — As you kindly promised me your visit for to-morrow afternoon, could you not make it convenient to stay and spend the evening with us? And would not your wife, Mr. and Mrs. Roche, Serena, Felix, and Clara join you then, and take tea with us? That arrangement would give great pleasure to Cécile and the children.

Now, I hope you all think as they do, and will say yes, and delight

Yours (in the singular and plural),

FELIX M. B.

This was the last note from the hand of Mendelssohn that Moscheles received. The days that the two friends should spend together on earth were numbered, but nothing foreboded the hour of separation that was so soon to strike. In Moscheles's diary we find daily memoranda of the usual friendly intercourse with Mendelssohn.

So on the 3d of October:—"In the afternoon we treated ourselves to some Fugues and Gigues of Bach's, and I was struck by Mendelssohn's intimate acquaintance with them. Then he gave us an imitation on the piano of a certain Polka which had been inflicted on him daily by a band of street musicians in Frankfurt. The trivial as well as the serious is food to his mind, and his impressions on all sides are turned to account in his compositions."

October 5.—"I spent the whole afternoon with Mendelssohn. He was pleased to see me, and we chatted confidentially on art and artists and Leipzig affairs generally. He played me a manuscript Quartet for string instruments in F minor, the four pieces of which are all in that sombre key. The impassioned character of the whole seems to me in keeping with his present frame of mind, shaken as he is to the heart's core by the loss of his sister."

October 7.—"Mendelssohn called to fetch me for a walk. In spite of the falling rain, we went to the Rosenthal, and time flew amid the most interesting conversations."

October 8.—"Examination of pupils for reception at the Conservatorio. Mendelssohn, who took an active part in the proceedings, tested them in thoroughbass and wrote out examples on the blackboard. Whilst they were at work, he sketched the most delightful landscapes—ever a creative genius! . . . Passed a most interesting afternoon and evening with Mendelssohn. He played his Violoncello Sonata in D major with Rietz, and the two Beethoven Sonatas, Op. 102; then my Sonate Symphonique with me."

On the following day, the 9th, another walk in the Rosenthal is recorded in the diary. It was a day not to be forgotten. Mendelssohn had much to tell of his last stay in England. He related the charming incidents of his visit to Queen Victoria and Prince Albert, and spoke of many mutual friends. At one o'clock he parted from the Moscheleses in the most cheerful mood; but it was only a few hours later that he was attacked by the illness from which he never recovered; and now followed days of anxiety and suspense, broken only by hopes that were not to be realized.

November 3. — "Mendelssohn better in the morning. In the afternoon another apoplectic stroke, depriving him of all consciousness. In the evening Charlotte and I, Madame Frege, David, and Schleinitz remained in the house till eleven o'clock."

"*Thursday, November* 4. — Before the day dawned my Felix had been to inquire, but could only bring us the most disheartening news."

The end was approaching. Moscheles's own words best describe the incidents of this, Mendelssohn's last day. In the anteroom of the death-chamber he wrote:[1] —

"Nature! demandest thou thy rights? Angels above, in heavenly spheres, do ye claim your brother whom ye regard as your own, as one too high for intercourse with us ordinary mortals? We still possess him, we still cling to him; we hope, by God's grace, to keep still longer amongst us one who has ever shone upon us, a pattern of all that is noble and beautiful, the glory of our century! To thee, O Creator, it is known why Thou hast lodged those treasures of heart and soul in so frail a tenement, that now threatens to dissolve! Can our prayers win from Thee the life of our brother? What a glorious work hast Thou

[1] Translated in "Life of Moscheles."

accomplished in him! Thou hast shown us how high he may soar heavenwards, how near he may approach Thee! Oh, suffer him to enjoy his earthly reward, — the blessings of a husband and father, the ties of friendship, the homage of the world!"

"*Noon.* — The doctors Hammer, Clarus, and Walther watch in turn by his bedside. Schleinitz writes out a bulletin that gives no hope. Dr. Frege and his wife and I are waiting anxiously near the sick-room. The doctors say that if no fresh attack on the nerves or lungs supervenes, the apparent calm may lead to a happy turn. . . .

"*Midnight.* — From two o'clock in the afternoon, at the hour when another paralytic stroke was dreaded, he gradually began to sink; he lay perfectly quiet, breathing heavily. In the evening we were all by turns assembled around his bed, contemplating the peaceful, seraphic expression on his countenance. The memory of that scene sank deeply into our hearts. Cécile bore up with fortitude under the crushing weight of her sorrow; she never wavered, never betrayed her struggle by a word. The children had been sent to bed at nine o'clock. Paul Mendelssohn stood transfixed with grief at the bedside of his dying brother. Madame Dirichlet and the Schuncks were expected in vain, — Dr. Härtel had travelled to Berlin to fetch them and Dr. Schönlein, but they could not arrive in time to witness the closing scene.

"From nine o'clock in the evening we expected

every moment would be the last; a light seemed to hover over his features, but the struggle for life became feebler and fainter. Cécile, in floods of tears, kneeled at his pillow; Paul Mendelssohn, David, Schleinitz, and I, in deep and silent prayer, surrounded his death-bed. As his breathing gradually became slower and slower, my mind involuntarily recurred to Beethoven's Funeral March, in the 'Eroica Symphony,' — to that passage where he seems to depict the hero, as he lies breathing his last, the sands of life gradually running out:

"The suppressed sobs of the bystanders and my own hot tears recalled me to the dread reality. . . . At twenty-four minutes past nine he expired with a deep sigh. The doctor persuaded the widowed Cécile to leave the room. I knelt down at the bedside, my prayers followed heavenwards the soul of the departed, and I pressed one last kiss on that noble forehead before it grew cold in the damp dew of death."

Moscheles remained in Leipzig, henceforth looking upon the Music School as on a precious heirloom, bequeathed to him by its founder; and during a period of twenty-three years — that is, until but a few days before his death in March, 1870 — he labored with untiring energy and devotion to instruct the rising generation of musicians, and to instil into their minds those artistic convictions and principles that had always been dear to him and to Mendelssohn.

INDEX.

INDEX.